TELEVISION
MANNA
FROM
HOLLYWOOD?

Quentin J. Schultze

Zondervan Books
Zondervan Publishing House
Grand Rapids, Michigan

TELEVISION: MANNA FROM HOLLYWOOD?
Copyright © 1986 by Quentin J. Schultze

Published by The Zondervan Corporation
Grand Rapids, Michigan

Zondervan Books is an imprint of Zondervan Publishing House,
1415 Lake Drive, S.E., Grand Rapids, Michigan 49506.

Library of Congress Cataloging in Publications Data

Schultze, Quentin J. (Quentin James), 1952–
  Television : manna from Hollywood?

  1. Television broadcasting—Religious aspects—Christianity. 2.
Television programs—United States. I. Title.
PN1992.6.S286   1986   260   86-19076
ISBN 0-310-27281-5

Edited by Pamela M. Hartung

Printed in the United States of America

86 87 88 89 90 91 / 10 9 8 7 6 5 4 3 2 1

Contents

Gratis

74970

Preface

I wrote this book for Christians who watch television. Parents, students, pastors, and educators will find it helpful as they struggle to use television constructively in their lives.

Television: Manna From Hollywood? differs from most other books about television in four important ways. First, I do not assume that television is inherently evil or part of a secular-humanist conspiracy. Although many programs are morally offensive and artistically inferior, some display clear evidence of God's grace. Television is not all bad; there are programs that we ought to enjoy and appreciate without feeling guilty. But too often we "watch television" instead of selecting programs. Christians are called to distinguish between worthwhile and worthless programs. To that task this book is addressed.

Second, this book is different in the way it evaluates television programs. Christians traditionally have criticized television only because of its immorality, especially its sexual immorality, giving our fellow human beings the impression that we are simply a cult of prudish media censors. From a Christian perspective, many shows are immoral. But such immorality hardly needs extensive description or evaluation; it's so blatant. This book is more concerned with the messages of the programs—what they say about human nature, truth, or love. Soap operas, for example, use various kinds of sexual innuendo to arouse viewers and hold their interest. But they also suggest that people are locked in a sometimes fierce struggle for survival; the only way for a person to get ahead is to use sinful power—coercion, blackmail, deception, seduction.

Third, instead of discussing specific programs, *Television: Manna From Hollywood?* addresses each of the major types of shows, from situation comedies to educational programs. It would be impossible to discuss all shows in depth in one book, and any book that attempted such a feat would be soon outdated. I use, as examples, only major programs that most Americans have seen either in their original run or in later syndication. Readers are encouraged to apply the ideas in the book to their favorite shows, even if they are not discussed here.

Fourth, this book looks at far more than television's effects on viewers. This medium is the major storyteller of our age. In spite of how seemingly trivial or silly most of the stories are, they reflect some of the basic beliefs of the people who watch them and the professionals who produce them. Programs are secular manna from Hollywood. Each chapter examines how spiritually nourishing various types of programs really are.

The last three chapters include specific suggestions for using television constructively in the home, school, and church. Readers who are faced with an immediate problem related to television viewing might want to read those chapters first.

I am indebted to the hundreds of scholars and researchers whose work I used in studying television and writing this book. The major points of the book are my own, however, and any comments should be directed only to the author.

TELEVISION: MANNA FROM HOLLYWOOD?

My students at Calvin College suffered through earlier drafts of this book in the form of lectures. I hope that they learned as much from me as I did from them. I am similarly indebted to the dozens of schools and churches whose teachers and congregations shared with me observations about television in their lives.

I always found the Zondervan staff pleasant and helpful. They are genuinely committed to serving Christ. Judith Markham helped me to clarify the concept for the book by reacting to early drafts. Pamela Hartung worked through the tedious but important manuscript editing process, helping to make the book readable. They both have my gratitude.

Linda Pott and Yvonne Posthuma, two marvelous secretaries, typed numerous drafts of the manuscript. They also made many helpful suggestions about style and organization. My colleague Randy Bytwerk cheerfully and fairly critiqued each chapter. His insight and good cheer made the final months of writing even pleasant. Conrad Bult and Stephen Lambers, along with other staff of the Calvin College Library, helped locate dozens of books and articles; they are members of an extremely helpful and dedicated college staff. David Holquist, chairman of my department, was a source of encouragement I needed especially during the dog days of summer, when the lure of Lake Michigan is too powerful to ignore.

My wife, Barbara, was the first to read each chapter. Her love was essential for completing this book, and her example in our home is the source of many of the constructive ideas offered in the last three chapters.

Quentin Schultze

1

Television in Our Lives

Fred Allen, the comic gen-
ius of early radio, once called television "chewing gum
for the eyes." Writer Michael J. Arlen similarly criticized
the medium: "Every civilization creates its own cultural
garbage and ours is television." Columnist Harriet Van
Horne quipped, "There are days when any electrical
appliance in the house, including the vacuum cleaner,
seems to offer more entertainment possibilities than the
TV set." There is a ring of truth in such epigrams. Many
programs are too ridiculous to take seriously. They are
frequently boring, idiotic, or simply silly, such as the
1969 wedding of Tiny Tim and Miss Vicki on "The
Tonight Show." Approximately 48 million viewers (one
of the largest audiences in the history of the show)
witnessed the couple exchange promises to be sweet,
gentle, kind, patient, and "not puffed up." The marriage
lasted a short time, but the publicity boosted Tiny's
career; he appeared on dozens of programs playing the

ukulele and singing falsetto versions of "Tiptoe Through the Tulips." If nothing else, television can turn unknown people into celebrities virtually overnight.

We all joke about how bad television is, but we still watch it. Almost half of all American adults tuned in to find out how "M*A*S*H" would end, and tens of millions stayed home to see who shot J.R. Our children are growing up on the visual food of "Mister Rogers" and "Sesame Street." Programs such as "Holocaust," "Roots," and "The Day After" directed public debate toward important social issues. Although quips about television's poor quality are always good for a laugh, they don't help us to understand how this medium influences our lives and how we might use it constructively.

Television is not the center of most people's lives, but it is nevertheless important. We now spend millions of dollars for satellite receivers, large-screen projectors, and videocassette recorders (VCRs)—not to mention the set itself. Television stations and satellite networks broadcast to 85 million American households on dozens of channels. If we include VCRs in our calculations, an increasing number of adults are spending more time watching television than any other leisure activity; during the fall of 1984, the average American adult for the first time spent more time watching television (fifty-two hours weekly) than working. Roughly speaking, the American lifestyle can be divided into three major activities: sleeping, working, and watching television. Because Americans watch so much television, they have made their nation's system of commercial broadcasting the most profitable and influential in the world.

Popular American shows are now broadcast around the free world, and copies of some programs are carried secretly across borders into Communist countries.

Television reaches into our personal lives. Parents name their children after television stars. College students gather in lounges to watch their favorite late-night show. Food producers peddle gourmet TV dinners. Truck dealers install sets in vans and motor homes. Husbands transform family rooms into bleachers on Sunday afternoons. Fans write to soap opera characters for help with personal problems. Hotels advertise waterbeds and X-rated cable television. "I hope we aren't becoming a nation of watchers," President Reagan once said in a public address, "because what made us great is that we have always been a nation of doers." Ironically, Reagan starred as host of one of television's successful westerns, "Death Valley Days."

VIEWING IT MORE BUT ENJOYING IT LESS

Surveys conducted over the last several decades offer two seemingly irreconcilable conclusions. On one hand, viewing has increased slowly but steadily since the medium's introduction in the late forties. In the average home the set is on about seven hours a day. On the other hand, surveys show that people are increasingly dissatisfied with television programming. Every year they complain that television has gotten a little worse; yet, each year they watch a little more. As the cigarette commercials used to proclaim about smoking, people are doing it more but enjoying it less.

How are we to account for such seemingly contradictory trends? First, we watch a lot of television because it's "free." Except for the initial cost of the set and occasional repair charge, commercial programs are free unless we subscribe to cable. The expenses of writing, producing, and distributing programs are passed along indirectly to viewers in the costs of advertised products. The price of every tube of toothpaste and package of gum includes a few cents to cover the costs of advertising and other marketing. As much as 20 percent of the retail price of some brands of cough medicine, for example, pays for advertising. Imagine what would happen to the size of the program audience if every set had a coin slot similar to those on soda pop machines. How thirsty for a sitcom would we have to be before reaching in our pockets for change? Would we pay a dollar for "M*A*S*H"? Five dollars? Would we pay more attention to what critics and friends tell us about particular shows? Would we plan our viewing more carefully? Probably so, given how carefully people select which films to see.

Cable television, which is available in about half of all American homes, shows how little people will actually pay for television programs. Most cable companies charge approximately ten dollars per month for twelve to one hundred channels. If the average household watched seven hours daily (the national average), each half-hour program would cost about four cents to watch. Still, millions of Americans apparently feel that cable is not worth the monthly charge.

Commercial television ensures that the networks will have high ratings, and it also affects how we view. If newspapers and magazine subscriptions were free, circulation would probably skyrocket. But how many subscribers would actually read their papers? In one out of five homes in which a television set is on, no one is in the room. Another 20 percent of the "viewers" are not likely to be paying attention to the program. They could be talking with a spouse, playing, reading, or making love, since the bedroom is the most likely place for a second television set.

We also watch a lot of television because it's so effortless. Reading a book or magazine, going to a film, and talking with friends all take more energy than watching a television program. Most of us place easy chairs or sofas in front of the set. Putting televisions in family rooms, kitchens, and bedrooms has helped make viewing a particularly casual and easy activity. It's amazing how a simple change of set location will affect viewing. For several years my wife and I kept our portable set in a closet and agreed that whoever took it out to view a show had to return it to its resting place. We quickly learned which programs were worth the effort; the set sometimes remained in the closet for weeks. When our children were toddlers, we moved the set to the family room and witnessed how quickly they began asking to watch various programs whenever they were bored. It was easier for them to turn on the tube than to play a game or to visit a friend down the block.

Primarily because television viewing is free and effortless, a few people actually become addicted; take away the television and they don't know what to do. Without the tube, such people find it difficult to carry on "normally." Admittedly, this type of addiction is not limited to television. Many people become professional hobbyists, devoting almost all of their leisure time to boating, stamp collecting, gardening, painting, and other enjoyable pastimes. Unlike many of these activities, however, watching television is often a substitute for sharing with others. Like playing video games and personal computing, excessive television watching can substitute for the rich personal friendships and warm fellowship that God wishes us to experience.

RING AROUND THE ADVERTISER

The blame for this state of affairs should not be placed solely on the viewers. History shows that television quickly became the most thoroughly commercialized mass-communication system in the world. Following in the footsteps of radio, the impressive technology of television was almost immediately transformed into a propaganda machine. Product manufacturers, advertising agencies, and the networks together made television the ideal medium for selling goods and services to mass audiences. The result was to anchor the medium in advertising, first through the sponsorship of such programs as "Texaco Theater," and later through half-minute commercials. In America television exists not primarily to inform or even to entertain people, but to attract the largest possible audiences. The commercial networks care less about how much someone enjoyed a show or whether society was improved by a program than about how well it did in the ratings.

CHRISTIANS RESPOND

Do Christians take television more seriously than others? Apparently not. Christians on average view the same amount of television as non-Christians; moreover, they tend to watch the same programs, except that believers tend to watch more religious broadcasts. Evangelicals may have distinctive views of Scripture and of the need for personal conversion, but they are as likely to watch a given soap opera or situation comedy as are people for whom Christ is merely a myth. Apparently, evangelicals' relationships to Christ have little or no impact on their television viewing.

This is surprising given evangelicals' traditional attitude toward "worldly amusements." Beginning with popular theater in the nineteenth century, many American denominations and preachers cautioned members that visual entertainment distracted believers from "higher things" and dulled their sensitivity to "spiritual matters." The rise of film in the early 1900s elicited similar warnings from clergy. A movie was "worldly" because it could be "antagonistic to vital piety," to use a phrase from one church report of 1924. The life of faith was deemed personal, somber, and print-oriented; the worldly life was seen as social, lighthearted, and visually oriented. The former symbolized personal piety; the latter, sinful self-indulgence.

By the time television came along in the late forties, most Protestant churches rejected simple categories to condemn the visual media, but evangelicals and other conservative Christians held a lingering suspicion of movies and television. As viewing became more commonplace in the home, they increasingly accepted it as harmless, even worthwhile. Evangelicals feared television content, especially the morality of particular scenes and programs, rather than television itself, which, they reasoned, was neither good nor bad. Each program, they felt, should be examined independently. Violent series, such as "Gunsmoke," were accepted only for adult viewing; variety programs, such as "The Ed Sullivan Show" and situation comedies like "Leave It To Beaver," were pronounced fit for family consumption. Finding such "redeeming" value in television, Christians eventually accepted it in the home.

Although they watched a lot of television, evangelicals remained suspicious of the medium. During the late seventies, the number of violent and sexually oriented scenes on television increased dramatically, and many Christians complained to the networks and sponsors. Younger Christians, who grew up with television in the home, were largely unconcerned; older Christians, however, felt betrayed, and their complaints were reminiscent of the worldly amusement fears voiced decades earlier. Changing social mores and attitudes toward sexuality were reflected in new shows, such as "All in the Family," "Soap," and "Three's Company." Television's moral standards had changed, but so had the nation's. Most Americans simply went along with the shifting mores.

Today Christians rarely call television a worldly amusement. Instead, they speak of its "immorality," which usually means its sexual explicitness, graphic violence, and profanity. There is no doubt that television writers and producers have been pushing televised sex to new limits in a quest for larger audiences. Nor is there any doubt that their strategy works. But Christian critics of the media frequently resemble prudish sin-hunters, looking at every show for violations of their personal moral standards. As we will see, television is more than portrayal of good or bad lifestyles, and it deserves more serious criticism by Christians.

MORALITY ON TELEVISION

Christians are rightly concerned with television's gratuitous sex and violence. Soap operas exploit human sexuality; many made-for-television movies are often written specifically to include sexual scenes and situations. Violence permeates the new action shows, which are filled with ricocheting bullets, automobile chases, and fights.

We err, however, by limiting morality to sex, violence, and profanity. Sexually related sins are not necessarily more severe than others. Our prudishness is evident in our frequent preoccupation with human sexuality and our relative disregard for sins related to greed, covetousness, and injustice. Television's general moral climate is far more evil than the few sexually explicit scenes would make us believe. What about lying, cheating, and stealing? What about disrespect for legitimate authority? What about racism and sexism? Are these not violations of God's moral codes? "All in the Family" was frequently criticized by Christians because of its profane language and sexual themes, such as Mike's impotence. Why were we not so critical of Archie's bigotry?

Morality on television is not just what some character does, but also the *point of view*. Everyone agrees that Archie Bunker defamed Jews in the various Norman Lear programs built around the character; J.R. Ewing of "Dallas" committed adultery. Both actions are sins. Did the programs condone Archie's bigotry and J.R.'s infidelity? Apparently so, since neither character was ever held accountable for his actions. Archie's prejudice only resulted in a few uncomfortable situations; J.R.'s adultery was part of an evil and unscrupulous way of life that won him power and prestige.

A program's point of view sets the context for viewers to evaluate characters' actions. In early television westerns, for example, evil gunslingers almost always met their death. The shows portrayed gunslinging not to glorify or encourage it, but to emphasize its fatal reward. Soap operas, on the other hand, give the viewer mixed clues regarding the sexual adventures of unmarried partners. The climate of soaps today is morally ambiguous. Sometimes virtue is rewarded; more frequently, the virtuous soap character is alienated and unfulfilled in spite of his actions. As we shall see, these changes in television's point of view reflect similar shifts in American values and attitudes.

Christians may disagree sometimes over a particular program's point of view. Even professional media critics offer widely divergent opinions about the same show. But let's not despair because of our disagreements. The important thing is for us to watch television with a critical Christian mind, to discuss programs with each other, and to adjust our viewing accordingly.

ART AND MORALITY

By focusing our attention too narrowly on sex and violence, we implicitly encourage the television industry to make artistically inferior programs. Even if program producers eliminated all immorality from their shows, the artistic quality of television drama would not be significantly improved; a morally unobjectionable program still might not be worth watching. If God is pleased by biblical points of view, He surely is pleased by programs that are well crafted, visually pleasing, and truly enjoyable to watch.

Many Christians praised "The Waltons" and "Little House on the Prairie" as excellent programs; but the lack of gratuitous sex and violence alone did not make them worthwhile series. Various artistic effects—the rich characterizations, the interesting stories, the relevant social and personal problems frequently addressed, the fine camera work—sometimes did. On the other hand, some episodes of these shows were predictable, historically inaccurate, and so corny they were laughable.

Christians should be the last to accept morally righteous but artistically inferior television shows, as we have so frequently done with Christian films and drama.

The quality of television drama varies from dreadful to excellent. Some programs are highly entertaining, while others are dull and repetitive. All of us have had the experience of not being able to recall what we watched on television the previous evening, or if we remember the name of the show, we often can't recall the plot. Such forgettable shows are probably a waste of time. We ought to feel disappointed and, in some cases, outraged over the quality of much of the drama that television networks promote as the "best" and "greatest" of each new season of programming. Television shows are sometimes a lot of hype and no substance.

I'm not suggesting that television drama ought to be limited to Shakespeare and other fine art productions, although I believe that much of the finest programming is on public television. Most drama written for the stage is a disappointment on television, in spite of the excellent attempts by television producers and directors to adapt it. Nevertheless, we should expect television to be reasonably good. Performers ought to be able to act; plots ought to make sense; settings ought to be appropriate; the camera ought to show us what's important in the story. As I will show in later chapters, sometimes even such basic artistic considerations are violated by program producers and television networks who care about little beyond the ratings.

TELEVISION AS STORYTELLER

Storytelling seems to be a universal trait of mankind. Every culture has its Iliads and Odysseys, its tales about great, courageous heroes, as well as its stories of tragic and pitiable characters. In today's world the daily paper is filled with news stories about the odd, interesting, and entertaining things people have done. Television commercials spin triumphal tales of lonely hearts who have found love apparently by using the right mouthwash or toothpaste. Sports magazines narrate the heroic actions of football heroes as well as the tragic tales of athletes whose careers were destroyed by drugs. We like stories, especially stories about people, and television is the major storyteller of our age.

Why do we enjoy stories? Some people believe that popular tales provide an escape from reality, a relief from the anxiety and conflict of our everyday lives. According to this theory, stories should be more popular when people are oppressed or despondent, such as during the Great Depression. But storytelling is far more than escape. A television program, for instance, can be a source of anxiety and fear. Shows about neighborhood crime may increase our concern about our own communities; medical dramas may cause us to think about our own health problems. Television not only removes us from the real world but also points us back to the day-to-day world we inhabit.

I believe that God also intends us to enjoy stories, including televised stories. We don't watch television only to escape from our daily routines. Nor do we always view television to be enlightened about the great issues of the day or solely to contemplate universal concerns of mankind. Much of storytelling is serious, intellectual, and even pedantic. But *all* storytelling should be enjoyable—for the storyteller as well as his audience. A well-told story pleases an audience, even if it is not an especially important one. For instance, a situation comedy, such as "Mary Tyler Moore" or "The Cosby Show," may never address the nature of evil, the problem of justice, or the existence of God, as some types of drama have throughout the ages. Yet the show might still be highly entertaining because of its interesting characters, unpredictable plots, and depictions of everyday life, such as raising teenagers.

Like most popular storytelling, television reaffirms our views of life. This has always been the major role of public storytelling in society. Consider the Old Testament Jews who used Passover and other holy days to tell the greatest stories of their history as a people. By retelling history, the Jews reaffirmed God's goodness to His people. Consider as well how contemporary Christians use the Bible to reaffirm their faith in God and their belief in His plan of redemption. Bible studies, worship services, personal devotions, and hymn sings are all occasions for reaffirming our faith, for recalling the stories of God's work in history.

Of course, television is not the Bible. Television is merely a medium; humans, not God, supply the stories. But in our age, television *functions* as the Bible for millions of people.

Imagine your family sitting comfortably in front of the television. First, you watch a situation comedy. Then, the children convince you to view an action show, such as the "A-Team" or "Dukes of Hazzard." Finally, the kids are off to bed, and you choose the latest episode of your favorite soap opera. Instead of gathering around the dinner table to retell the Passover story, you have shared dramatic tales of three common types of programs—a sitcom, an action show, and a serial.

TELEVISION: MANNA FROM HOLLYWOOD?

Each genre tells a particular kind of story. All sitcoms are basically the same. So are most westerns and detective shows. The characters and settings may differ, but the structure and message of each program are typically similar. Later, we will look at the structure of each of the major television genres to see how television uses age-old formulas to reaffirm basic beliefs, held by Christians and non-Christians alike.

Television is the most popular mythology of a diverse people, so it tends to confirm those beliefs common to the masses. We watch television, in part, expecting to have our beliefs reaffirmed, not to learn something new or to see and hear the unexpected. We assume the good guys will win and the bad guys will be brought to justice. We also anticipate that the goodness of human beings will be evident, as in the reconciliation among characters at the end of a situation comedy.

Of course life is not exactly as our favorite program portrays it. Nor is the point of view of every show the same as our personal perspective on the world. Television reaffirms our society's basic beliefs, but it is also at odds with what many of us know to be the truth. This book examines that tension between the world of television and the truths of scripture. Thanks to the grace of God, television sometimes captures aspects of the Creation and Fall, and even something of the joy of living under the Redemption. More often programs are morally, artistically, and spiritually bankrupt. In either case, our look at the great popular storyteller will help us understand the culture in which we live, the manna that both nourishes and starves us.

2

Children's Television:
Baby-sitting the Kids

In the permanent collection of the Smithsonian Institution in Washington, D.C., hangs the most famous red sweater in the history of mankind. It's not the sweater of a president, or any other dignitary, but of a humble, soft-spoken Presbyterian minister from rural Pennsylvania. His name is Fred Rogers, better known as Mister Rogers of the well-known program on public broadcasting. One of the cardigans knitted by his mother and worn during tapings of the show, "the sweater is the most obvious, visible symbol of Mister Rogers. It's his trademark, his costume," said one of the museum's curators.

American broadcasting has given the nation hundreds of popular children's programs and heroes, beginning with Buffalo Bob of "Howdy Doody." During the early years of television, shows like "Kukla, Fran and Ollie," "Bozo the Clown," and "Captain Kangaroo" were seen by millions of young Americans. Unlike today's programs for youngsters, these simple shows were usually broadcast live in front of a studio audience.

During the fifties children's television became a big business for the networks, who changed radically the ways of writing and producing shows for young people. Drama replaced circus and puppet acts, leading to shows like "My Friend Flicka," "Adventures of Robin Hood," and "Tales of the Texas Rangers." These dramatic productions lured even more children to the television set.

The advent of color television in the sixties provided producers with the most attractive vehicle yet for garnering large audiences of children—the animated cartoon. Yogi Bear, Fred Flintstone, Bugs Bunny, and dozens of other characters became household words as many kids and parents watched prime-time cartoons. Other parents were uneasy about cartoons, citing the amount of violence on most of them. Eventually cartoons were shifted to Saturday mornings, where few adults viewed them.

Then, public television inaugurated "Sesame Street," a mixture of studio drama, animated cartoon, and short films, dubbed by its creators as "educational casting." PBS followed with a series of other educational programs funded by local public stations, viewers, private corporations, and the government. "Sesame Street" and its offshoots met with a few critics, but the majority of Americans welcomed the new style of program for their youngsters. Few parents doubted any longer; most found that at least some television programs were worthwhile even for their preschool children.

During the eighties, however, parents' criticism of television increased once again as the commercial networks turned to a new type of show—the semiserious action show, such as "A-Team." It seemed that the networks were no longer committed to making prime-time programs specifically for children; instead, they hoped to produce adult drama that attracted young people. Once again many parents complained about the amount of violence on these shows with little effect. "A-Team" and its imitators successfully attracted audiences, which in commercial television is the major consideration.

As the business of children's television has grown over the years, the programs have become increasingly violent, visually enticing, and hero-worshiping. What can parents do to control the influence of these shows on their children? Are some programs better than others for youngsters? Should children have such larger-than-life television heroes? Are gun-slinging commandos and self-appointed lawmen the role models for the future?

CHANGING LIFESTYLES

Children's programs in the United States and Canada are popular partly because of changing lifestyles and family structures. Television is a medium for the middle class, and children's shows historically have catered to the tastes and ideals of middle-class families, who think of television as a way of passing time. Television is meant to be *watched*, they assume, not to be viewed critically. Children and their parents have made television the nation's major leisure activity, surpassing sports, games, and even conversation.

Surveys show that most parents don't examine seriously the role that television should play in their family. Of course we're concerned on occasion with excessive television violence and explicit sexual portrayals, but as long as the set displays unobjectionable images, we're content to let the children enjoy their favorite programs. After all, we like our prime-time soap operas and sports programs as much as the kids enjoy their Saturday morning cartoons.

By labeling television as an unimportant leisure activity, parents frequently rationalize irresponsible viewing. We allow preschoolers to see their favorite cartoons without supervision on Saturday morning so we can catch up on needed sleep—sleep required often because of a late television movie that kept us up the night before. We permit two-year-olds to watch prime-time action shows with their older siblings so we can relax for an hour on the patio with the neighbors. We assume that "Sesame Street" and the other educational programs are always good for our children, knowing that any alternative to watching television would require more work on our part. Kids need attention, we admit, but why not let them get it from Big Bird and Oscar the Grouch?

As middle-class Christians, our lifestyles are often patterned not after the lordship of Christ, but after the veneration of leisure promoted by commercials and programs. Relaxation is an important, God-given activity for mankind; all adults and children need to strengthen the recreational dimensions of their lives, giving glory to the Creator, who rested on the seventh day of the Creation. But when leisure becomes selfish action, when we justify our own rest and recreation at the expense of our children, the family suffers. Parents have become increasingly involved in their own favorite pastimes, sometimes neglecting to teach Godly leisure to their children through instruction and example.

The situation is worsened by divorce and the growing

number of families where both parents are employed full time. Single parents have an enormous responsibility to make a living and raise a family, so television easily becomes a surrogate spouse, keeping the children occupied while essential household chores are completed. And many two-parent families, caught up in the ideals of material success, send both parents into the work force while the children gather around the set before and after school. In both types of homes, television is not usually a planned leisure activity, but a seemingly inescapable mechanism for adapting to contemporary lifestyles.

Children's television is aptly named because it usually separates children from the rest of the family rather than bringing the family together. Preschool children spend, on an average, approximately thirty hours each week watching television, less than three hours of which are viewed with either parent. Even parents of children over six years of age spend only about three hours per week viewing programs with their school-age offspring. Has television become the baby-sitter, the electronic nanny that is teaching children a view of the world opposed to the lordship of Christ?

EDUCATIONAL TELEVISION

In a broad sense all television educates our children. Values, attitudes, and behaviors are part of almost all programming, from cartoons to prime-time adventure shows. It's difficult to determine what children actually *learn* from any particular program, but at least they see and hear what characters are doing and saying. Television characters apparently can affect a child's self-image because kids compare themselves with program heroes, hoping to be like their favorite ones and even imitating their particular behaviors. In rare cases adolescents have murdered and raped after seeing depictions of such violent acts on a home set. Most parents, however, don't think of such television effects as education, since 76 percent of them say that "education" is the medium's major *benefit* for children.

Parents and educators speak of "educational television" as those programs, usually aired on the public broadcasting system, made specifically to develop intellectual or cognitive abilities, such as recognizing numbers and letters. Are programs such as "Sesame Street" and "Mister Rogers' Neighborhood" really educational? Should parents provide unlimited access to such shows for their children?

In recent years probably no program has been more popular with preschool children than "Sesame Street." Approximately ten million two- to five-year-olds watch it regularly, along with six million older children and ten million adults. Yet few parents realize that the show was started in 1968 as a two-year experiment to give children from disadvantaged homes an introduction to school—a kind of televised preschool. As one of the creators of "Sesame Street" said, the program was based on the principle that "entertainment could be a useful vehicle for education." "Sesame Street" was meant to make learning fun for children from low-income, urban homes by imitating many of the production techniques used in television commercials. Creators of "Sesame Street" never envisioned the program as daily entertainment for middle-class kids in suburban areas, which is largely what it became by the mid-seventies. Oscar, Big Bird, Grover, and the rest of the "Sesame Street" cast are indeed popular with middle-class America, but there is little evidence that the show significantly educates the nation's children. Its success has always been judged more on the basis of its popularity than actual learning.

Rapid-fire visual changes, catchy musical jingles, and animated characters are the stock-in-trade of both "Sesame Street" and the typical half-minute television advertisement. The program captures a child's attention for precisely the same reasons that one television commercial can capture the attention of a living room full of noisy preschoolers engaged in other playful activities. The product sold on "Sesame Street" is a letter or a number instead of a pack of chewing gum or the latest battery-operated, remote-controlled army tank.

The question for parents is whether the commercial techniques used on "Sesame Street" justify the little learning that actually takes place. A study funded a number of years ago by the Russell Sage Foundation concluded that "six months viewing of 'Sesame Street' led to little cognitive gain" in preschoolers. Although children may find the program very entertaining and may even "learn" something—no one knows precisely what—they will probably not gain much intellectually from even daily viewing of Oscar and the rest of the gang. Over the years "Sesame Street" producers have changed the program's goals somewhat to include improved self-esteem and emotional and social development, but there is little evidence that the program's format is well suited for such educational goals.

Although it's impossible to measure the long-term effects of viewing "Sesame Street," the show's visual razzle-dazzle and frenetic pace may actually make it more difficult for preschoolers to adjust to the comparatively simple appearance and leisurely tempo of the typical kindergarten class. Youngsters may actually learn through the show that learning itself is entertaining and fun, when much of learning is actually hard work and self-discipline; there are few classroom teachers who could compete with an eight-foot canary or a grouchy character who pops out of a garbage can. With the best of intentions, the creators of "Sesame Street" successfully produced a format that holds the attention of millions of the nation's preschool children, but the program was never meant to be so successful. Perhaps middle-class America will be the victim of its popularity.

THE MORAL NEIGHBORHOOD
OF MISTER ROGERS

If "Sesame Street" teaches that learning and entertainment are indistinguishable from each other, "Mister Rogers' Neighborhood" teaches that human beings should love one another. The "neighborhood," of course, is mankind, and Fred Rogers daily invites young viewers to his home, where the world's problems and complexities are addressed with childlike simplicity. Through the "land of make-believe," to which the children are ushered by a clanging red trolley, and visits with other members of the neighborhood, Rogers carefully conveys his message: all people are worthy of love and respect.

The theme of the show is nowhere more evident than in Rogers' own program format. Whereas "Sesame Street" manipulates the viewer through visual razzle-dazzle, Rogers' program moves along slowly and carefully, letting each child take in the music, talk, and play at his own pace. To the adult and the older child raised on television, Rogers' character is dull and uninteresting, since he seems like a wimpy bore whose lack of machismo should have kept him off the tube. But to the young child not yet influenced by the jaundiced eye of television, Rogers is a father and friend. Rogers' aim is not to adjust the child to the visually manipulative demands of television, but to adjust television to the cognitive level and emotional needs of the child.

Ironically, Rogers' television career began at a commercial network, where he assisted in producing such shows as "Your Lucky Strike Hit Parade" and "The Kate Smith Hour." But after working his way up to network floor director, he left New York for the fledgling public station in Pittsburgh, WQED-TV, where he started his first children's program in 1954. Eventually he created "Misterogers," a fifteen-minute program broadcast by the Canadian Broadcasting Corporation. Meanwhile he attended seminary classes on his lunch hour and was ordained a Presbyterian minister in 1963. With the inauguration of "Mister Rogers' Neighborhood" in 1964, two of Fred Rogers' childhood dreams had come true: a seminary degree and a network program specifically for children.

Rogers' background in television production, his religious faith, and his understanding of child development combine to provide him with special insight into how to use a visual medium to communicate his message of love and acceptance. Free from the financial shackles of commercial broadcasting, he has experimented with program techniques that appear boring and stilted to the average adult viewer but are of great benefit to children when parents watch and discuss it with them. Rogers' programs sometimes deal with issues and problems of great complexity and importance—war, divorce, child care—and these are matters that require the support and love of the parents, not simply the reassuring voice of Fred Rogers emanating from the television set. We should be thankful that public broadcasters and the Sears Foundation have supported Rogers' work over the years. But what about the role of parents in the lives of their children? Who should they be learning love and acceptance from?

THE CARTOON CAPER

Many parents associate the term "children's television" with the Saturday morning cartoons broadcast on the major commercial networks. But are these cartoons really produced for children? And what is their influence on our youngsters?

The networks began broadcasting cartoon programs in the sixties because they were inexpensive to make and because a growing number of advertisers wanted to reach the "children's market." Cereal and toy makers lined up to sponsor such programs, and program makers responded by developing a new assembly-line technology for producing animated cartoons that eliminated the need for hundreds of drawings. Bugs Bunny, Yogi Bear, and the rest of the cartoon characters jumped across television sets during the early hours of prime-time programming, after supper but before the children were put to bed. Eventually the networks led the sponsors to Saturday morning, which was filled with endless reruns and a few new cartoons.

Because the early cartoons were aired during evening hours, the programs were written for all ages. "The Flintstones," for example, was little more than an animated version of "The Honeymooners," the early domestic situation comedy starring Jackie Gleason. Fred

Flintstone's cave resembled the Kramden's apartment, and Fred's voice imitated Jackie Gleason's. "Rocky and His Friends" included segments called "Fractured Fairy Tales" and "Bullwinkle's Corner," a poetry reading by the dim-witted moose. Other cartoons contained material similarly above the heads of most young children.

Common belief is that cartoons are for kids, but the old-style cartoons were never really written specifically for children, let alone for preschoolers. Cartoons initially dealt with adult themes and relied on adult humor—the ceaseless stalking of the roadrunner by the coyote, the adventures of the suave pink panther, the romantic escapades of Pepe Le Peu. Although cartoons are enjoyed by many children, they were not written with the cognitive, moral, and social needs of children in mind.

Children like cartoons because of their action. The repeated bumpings, bouncings, and bashings are visually seductive to the young child, who inhabits the comparatively unstimulating visual environment of the home. It should come as no surprise, then, that cartoons replaced the highly violent action-adventure programs of the fifties. Under public and congressional pressure resulting from the federal hearings on television violence, the networks dropped after-school programming, turning the time slot over to the local stations. By the late sixties, however, violence reappeared in the seemingly benign form of the "kids' cartoon." History shows that cartoons were a clever and profitable way for the networks to make violent programming more palatable to the American public.

There is no strong evidence that cartoon violence is less violent or harmful than violence depicted on shows with "real" people playing the roles of dramatic characters. Children under eight years of age are very confused about what on television is *real* and what is merely *make-believe*. They don't usually comprehend plot, so they can't put violence into the context of a program's overall theme or message. Through about second grade, children perceive television as little more than people doing interesting things, not narratives about life or about people. Children of this age also understand little of the visual techniques used by television directors and cartoon animators. While parents can help their children to understand cartoon stories, few parents take the time to watch these kinds of shows and discuss them as a family. As a result, cartoons have little redeeming value for young children. Parents who think that the "moral" of a Smurf or Strawberry Shortcake program makes the show worthwhile are simply fooling themselves. The cartoon with a good moral assuages the concerned parent, but it does little for the young child who watches it.

During the early eighties, local stations introduced a new style of afternoon cartoon specifically designed to attract children and sell them toys. The most successful of the new cartoons, "He-Man and the Masters of the Universe," helped Mattel, Inc. in the first two years to sell over $500 million of He-Man toys and another $500 million of He-Man toothbrushes, underwear, sheets, alarm clocks, and other products manufactured under license to Mattel. Soon other toy makers introduced feature-length cartoons, Saturday morning series, and holiday specials featuring animated versions of their new products. Toy industry guidelines prevented manufacturers from advertising their toys during a show featuring the characters but did not prevent them from creating a desire for their toys.

SELLING THE KIDS

Just as young children do not comprehend the nature of cartoons and other types of televised stories, they are also confused about the purpose of the half-minute commercial. Children under nine years of age often can distinguish between an advertisement and a program, but they aren't able to understand the selling intent of an advertisement without help from an older child or adult. In most cases a commercial is more exciting and interesting than the show, partly because of the visual techniques used by advertisers and partly because of the children usually participating in the commercial. Kids like to watch other kids on television. It's easy for parents to conclude that their youngster "understands" commercials, but chances are that the child merely understands that it's not the program.

One of the greatest tragedies of American television is that it has turned children into simply another audience to be sold to advertisers. Programs are written and produced primarily to attract young viewers, not fundamentally to educate, enlighten, or even entertain. The networks, of course, equate entertainment with ratings, but this is like saying that the most popular teacher is also the best or that the top-selling automobile is the most reliable.

If we allow our children to watch commercial television, we must also be prepared to deal sensitively yet forcefully with the influence of advertisements. We cannot ignore commercials because they are really the most persuasive and manipulative of all forms of popular storytelling. They wheedle, cajole, and mystify our children with the hope of a better life in the latest toy,

33

candy, or cereal. Above all, they entertain in their own carefully researched ways, from the circus atmosphere of McDonalds to the romantic stirrings of the Barbie-doll commercial. Taken as a whole, commercials are designed to turn our children into committed consumers. Regardless of the product advertised, the commercial message is the same—desire.

So, the task of the Christian parent is raising children who seek first the kingdom of God, not the most realistic doll or the latest model car. Covetousness is one of the greatest sins of our age. As C. S. Lewis suggests in *The Screwtape Letters*, in modern society Satan scores victories by giving people what they want. Give them a nice, comfortable life, a closet full of designer clothes, and the latest, fastest automobile. Greed accelerates and faithlessness blossoms. Modern advertising flies so directly into the face of the tenth commandment that it is remarkable how complacent American Christians are about the consumer culture in which they live. Advertising is effective with our children partly because we cherish its message in our own hearts and give credence to it in our parental behavior.

PARENTING IN A TELEVISION AGE

In the last half-century, radio and television have taken over some of the functions of church, school, and family. Our children are socialized partly by the endless barrage of sounds and pictures emanating from the latest electronic gadgets, from credit-card-sized stereo radios to the new breed of low-priced video-cassette recorders. While parents chase the good life, their children uncritically watch programs designed to attract viewers and maximize advertising revenues. Do we really want the networks to raise our children? Obviously not, so the important question for all parents is how to raise children in a television age.

The impact of children's programs is determined largely by the role of parents in setting standards for using television in the home. Parents who give their children free rein of the television, who use television thoughtlessly as a baby-sitter, are making the set into a surrogate parent. Parents, on the other hand, who help their children decide what to watch and even discuss the programs with their kids are likely to reap educational and spiritual benefits for the entire family. Television viewing is actually an opportunity for parents to teach their children by example and loving discussion. If Christ is actually Lord of our lives, we ought to show it in the programs we watch and the ones we permit our kids to see.

Communication between parent and child is crucial in building strong, rewarding family relationships, and television programs are one potential topic for discussion. "Mister Rogers' Neighborhood" and other shows for preschoolers frequently address issues of social concern to all families: anger, death, divorce, friendship. Even "Sesame Street" in recent years has increased the number of shows on themes of interest to children and parents. But such "educational" programs lose most of their value without parental guidance and loving support. These shows can be important opportunities for parents to initiate discussions with their youngsters; when children watch such programs alone, however, the benefit is largely lost because television becomes an impersonal parent. Children need to learn and discuss life with a real person with whom they can interact spontaneously. Then, this kind of discussion turns some of television's wasteland into a worthwhile experience for the entire family.

As growing children lose interest in programs created for preschoolers, they move on to action programs, game shows, cartoons, sitcoms, and whatever else interests them. They begin using television heroes as role models, acting out in the home the situations and violent acts depicted on the television set. Cartoons are still of interest but not always as appealing now as the more realistic action shows, such as "Dukes of Hazzard" and "A-Team." Even the growing child's interest in commercials shifts from specifically children's products to ads for mass market items, such as soda pop and potato chips, to more expensive adult items including cars and clothes. Children are often fascinated with the ways such adult products are portrayed; commercials are for them often a peek into the world of grown-ups—a peek sponsored by Madison Avenue. While five-year-olds are far from reaching adulthood, thanks largely to television they stand on the threshold of becoming bona fide American consumers.

By seven or eight years of age, watching television becomes a very important part of children's lives, unless parents involve them in activities outside of the home. This is the crucial period for introducing children to hobbies that will enhance their self-esteem and teach them social skills. Sports activities, reading clubs, and musical groups offer opportunities for intellectual, social, and moral development. Regular classroom work is important, but it is not enough; children need to become involved in voluntary activities that ease them into new social experiences and friendships. This is also a good time for parents to bring children with them to civic occasions, public activities, and church meetings. American children, in particular, need to experience other cultures, since television, like society in general, is such an ethnocentric institution.

BOOKS AND TELEVISION

In spite of the educational benefits of some programs for children, television for the most part does not point children toward the world of books. Even shows designed to teach reading skills, such as "The Electric Company," don't interest children in the beauty and importance of words. Video equipment and computers in the classroom have not changed the literary character of schooling. The written word is still the foundation of learning, and it is very unlikely that television viewing alone significantly contributes to a child's interest in reading or to his reading ability.

Some educators believe that all television viewing decreases students' interest in novels, textbooks, and even popular publications such as newspapers and magazines. They may be right, but there is also evidence that television viewing is not the only rascal. Socioeconomic factors, such as family income and educational level, are better predictors of children's reading skills than television viewing. Moreover, some studies have shown that students who don't watch television generally do not score as well on achievement tests as students who watch a limited amount of television. One study even found that children who regularly watch one of the major religious programs on cable do poorer in school.

The message for parents is clear: Even so-called educational television programs will not automatically cultivate good reading habits and lead to high academic achievement. But they should not blame television solely for a child's poor performance in school. As most teachers know, the public schools in urban areas are struggling with financial and discipline problems, so we should not be surprised that socioeconomic factors are better predictors of school performance than television viewing. The quality of our schools and the atmosphere of the home are extremely important in encouraging a child's interest in the printed page. Neither unlimited television viewing nor the elimination of television will ensure that American children receive a worthwhile education.

Relationships between parents and their children are critical in developing academically superior students. If parents themselves read, and if they read regularly to their children, it is very likely that their children will also become readers. Presently the average adult in the United States spends over one thousand hours in front of the television set every year but spends only about five hours reading books—a grim situation. While we don't wish to idolize reading, making it superior to all other human activities, we must admit that the knowledge and pleasure derived from books are gifts from God worth preserving. What kind of example do we set for our children? Do they see in our habits an appreciation of the gift of books? Or do our children see in us a hypocrisy that preaches the importance of school but lives without reading?

Parents of young children should be especially concerned about preserving the ritual of family readings. A child who associates the warmth of a parent's body and the assurance of a parent's voice with the reading of stories is well on the way to becoming a lover of books. The cold glow of the television set can't compete with the comforting sounds of a mother's or father's voice if the latter is given a chance to work its spell in the home. Family devotions are not enough because our concern is with literary as well as spiritual development.

Once children are involved in worthwhile activities outside of the home, the lure of the television set is far less compelling. They are less apt to sit passively in front of a picture tube for hours watching others talk instead of communicating with neighbors, friends, and new acquaintances.

After all, Christ blessed and received the children. Young ones are special creatures in God's sight, and they should be in ours as well. To best serve our children, we must become childlike ourselves, experiencing and celebrating the wonder of God's Creation as reflected in our own offspring.

3

Soap Operas: Survival of the Fittest

During the early days of radio, they were called washboard weepers, sudsers, and soap operas. Today, the television versions are known simply as "soaps," and the dozen or so aired daily are watched by a growing number of Americans. Daytime soaps alone are viewed by a total of 20 to 30 million people. Surprisingly, 15 percent of viewers are male. A recent study of college students found that half of them watch daytime television serials. Other studies have determined that soap viewers are representative of the entire nation. Now programs such as "Dallas" and "Dynasty" have successfully introduced soaps on prime-time television all over the world.

Soaps have shown an amazing ability to weather the ratings storms of commercial broadcasting. Most prime-time series today last only one viewing season, and nervous network executives cancel some shows after only four episodes. In comparison, some of the currently popular soaps have lasted for decades. "Love of Life" ended twenty-eight years of television in 1980, which made it the longest-running episode show on American television.

There are soap-opera festivals, fan clubs, magazines, books, and newsletters. Program producers distribute their shows in Great Britain, Australia, and the Continent. Evening soaps, such as "Dallas," have attracted a large following in foreign countries, as they have in the United States.

WHY ARE SOAPS SO POPULAR?

Soaps are popular partly because of the vicarious involvement of viewers in the lives of program characters. Robert E. Short, manager of daytime programs for Proctor and Gamble Productions, says, "For the most part, women tend to look at these shows not as programs but as friends; these characters are people they know like neighbors and they come in to visit with them every day. They develop an extreme loyalty to characters that they care about; they identify with them and enjoy watching them." Such active identification is encouraged by fan magazines, clubs, and the television network's own promotional activities. Some viewers send birthday and anniversary cards, and occasionally gifts to program characters. Actors are stopped on the street by viewers who mistake them for the characters they portray. Of course, soap writers intentionally create strong viewer involvement by dramatizing important personal occasions. Two of the highest-rated daytime soap audiences ever recorded were weddings on "General Hospital" and "All My Children."

Soaps are also popular because of their devoted use of

the cliff-hanger to leave the audience wondering what will happen next. Charles Dickens and others used this technique in nineteenth-century literature. Now soap writers have even adapted it to prime-time television, providing minor cliff-hangers at the end of each episode, and major cliff-hangers at the conclusion of each television season. Viewers watch soaps in anticipation of an end to the story, so it's easy to get "hooked" on a particular soap.

MORALITY TO AMBIGUITY

The daytime radio serial first merited the name "soap opera." These programs, started in the thirties, were episodic, moralistic, and domestic. In "Soapland," James Thurber described the typical radio soap: "Between thick slices of advertising, spread twelve minutes of dialogue, add predicament, villainy and female suffering in equal measures, throw in a dash of nobility, sprinkle with tears, season with organ music, cover with a rich announcer sauce, and serve 5 times a week."

The first television soaps were patterned after the successful radio serials. Some of them, such as "Guiding Light," were merely transferred from radio to the new visual medium, with the same actors playing other major parts. Scripts were initially altered only to provide television producers and directors with enough information to enable them to guide the performance before the cameras. Later, technical improvements were introduced: the use of color, detailed sets, on-location shots, four and five camera set-ups, videotaping, more attention to costumes and make-up. Such improvements were partly an attempt to make daytime drama look more like prime-time television. Less apparent to viewers was a gradual shift in the genre's stories and characters.

SOAP OPERAS: SURVIVAL OF THE FITTEST

Television soaps progressively removed the moralistic shackles of radio serials to better reflect the mixed-up social mores and contradictory values of modern America. Old-fashioned virtues were silly and obsolete, according to soap writers, and they began producing the kinds of stories that would attract young viewers who no longer believed that the practice of simple virtues would lead to a happy and rewarding life. They used obviously "good" and "bad" events and characters—the evil seductress, the stable and loving mother, the wicked womanizer; these story elements, however, were not promoting particular moral themes. No longer are virtuous actions always rewarded; no more do most soaps portray the benefits of personal frugality, faith, or fidelity. Most contemporary soaps are not moralistic. There simply is too much chaos, too many loose ends, and far too much moral ambiguity to warrant the belief that soaps are old-fashioned promoters of virtue.

Today we find on the soaps a world of chance and uncertainty. Adultery, divorce, and premarital sex abound, and there appears to be no way of determining when such activities are justified and when they are not. Good characters get caught in bad situations. Conversely, good things happen to bad characters. Well-intentioned actions sometimes boomerang, so that virtuous actions appear to serve no good purpose. Characters are lonely, hurting, and depressed because of what others have done to them. They are unsure about what to do with their lives and must constantly seek the advice of other similarly confused characters. There are peeks at happiness and virtue, but they are almost always fleeting. Soap-opera characters are players in a mixed-up game of life where no one is sure of the rules or the purpose, so they must make them up as they go along.

NO PLACE FOR HEROES

Soap operas are the slowest-moving genre on television. They move so slowly, former viewers can sometimes be filled in on the last year's happenings in only a few minutes. Whereas most television drama emphasizes action, soaps deal in anticipation. Where there is little action, there cannot be great heroes. Heroes need something to accomplish.

Most soap-opera episodes are filled with dialogue. Characters are constantly talking about their problems and the problems of their friends, relatives, and enemies. They argue, discuss, reveal, plead, disagree, converse, and chat. But to what end? By the time one crisis is averted, others are anticipated. The result is a genre that exudes hopelessness. Characters typically appear unable to act upon the world, to make it a better place to live, or to change it for the good. They are ineffective, powerless, and helpless. And there are no heroes to save them.

Compare the soap opera with the typical prime-time action program, such as "Dukes of Hazzard" or "A-Team." In the latter, characters accomplish something. They learn of a crime, for instance, and catch the criminals. By comparison, the soap-opera character is caught in a web of relationships and conflicts far too complex and changeable to be significantly improved. Change occurs, but it is typically outside of the control of any particular characters. Divorces, for example, seem almost inevitable; if a divorce is forestalled, it is usually not a result of the efforts of particular characters.

Soaps lack a main figure—a protagonist—whose actions would reveal to the audience the significance of the drama. Viewers are treated instead to a hodgepodge of weak characters motivated by self interest at worst and shallow love at best. Viewers usually like one character more than another, but such affection is not based on characters' heroic or villainous qualities. Avid viewers say of their favorite characters, "He's cute!"; "She's a jerk."; "Isn't so and so sweet?" These are not the qualities of heroes or villains, but of weak and unimportant characters. In the great majority of soaps, to drop any character from the story would not change appreciably the nature and theme of the program. If no character has the power to resolve the conflict, if no character may act to bring the story to its conclusion, there are no soap heroes.

Love is also strangely absent from most soap operas. One would expect, given the genre's preoccupation with romance, that self-sacrificing love would frequently motivate characters. Instead, soaps are filled with selfish and egocentric persons who are more concerned with satisfying their own needs and fulfilling their own desires. Apparently love is too risky for the typical soap character; self-sacrifice makes one too vulnerable to others, who may take advantage of the situation. Life on the soaps is too uncertain and potentially cruel for selfless love.

Soap characters are forever caught in the storms of life, trying to maintain emotional stability in an unstable, unpredictable world. Some characters' lives improve for a time, but both characters and viewers know that trials and tribulations are around the corner. The future cannot be known, and in spite of characters' attempts to mold it, they know that the future is out of their grasp. The soap world is a cruel place.

God's grace rarely appears in soaps. They offer few

glimpses into how the storms of life might be related to some eternal purpose, let alone some sense of ultimate beginning and end. The cosmic dimensions of history are reduced to the here and now: Joanne and Bob are not getting along, Jessica fears an end to her affair with Sean, James plots how to seduce Kay. Only the mystery of chance transcends the daily struggles of characters.

Happiness for the typical soap-opera character is merely the absence of interpersonal conflict and strife. There is little satisfaction with life or personal fulfillment. The most they may hope for is temporary peace—time away from the turmoil created by selfish people and lady luck. It is usually the older characters— often on their death bed—who are finally shielded from the wounding words and actions of others. Only then is there time to ponder the meaning of life and to "find one's inner strength." Work, too, is rarely a source of personal pride or vocational accomplishment, but primarily a way to *make a living*. This is true of even the wealthiest professionals on the daytime serials; work gets in the way of personal goals of power and sex.

Daytime television serials portray the world as a Darwinian struggle for survival: Characters are born, live, and die. Some "make it"—socially, financially, psychologically, sexually—and others do not. It is a drama of characters chasing characters, predators hunting their prey. Each character is striving to make it to the next episode unscathed or, with a bit of luck, to improve his standing among competitors. In one of the craziest plot shifts of the soaps, the character of Laura on "General Hospital" falls in love with Luke, who had raped her a year before. Some characters master their rivals, but their struggle for happiness and stability in the ever-changing soap world will eventually lead once again to pain, rejection, loneliness, or fear. Rarely is there joy or unabashed humor in a soap opera.

Soap operas are popular partly because they mirror some of the most fundamental myths of modern society. The genre reflects an evolutionary naturalism in which human society is a collection of animalistic individuals battling for survival. There is no God and no place for transcendent values from a god. Humankind is stranded on this earth and locked in a struggle. Perhaps the soap opera is best viewed as a human version of a typical animal-nature program, such as Mutual of Omaha's long-running series "Wild Kingdom." Just as the nature program tells stories of animal adaptation and survival, soaps spin tales of human struggles. Nature programs personify animals while soaps turn people into animals.

Some Christians have argued that the only problem with soap operas is that they lack a few God-fearing characters. This view of soaps doesn't recognize how the theme of survival fits the genre regardless of the types of characters used. "Religious" soap characters are caught in the same struggle for survival as other characters. Their faith in God becomes merely one more way of adapting to the social environment. Such characters "use" religion just as nonbelieving characters use their own strategies to survive. Who is to say that religion is any more effective at guaranteeing survival than flattery, blackmail, and murder? Only if, for the Christian, life has no ultimate significance, no relationship to a beginning and an end, can the soap opera be made into "Christian drama." Because humankind is part of a created cosmic order, the soap opera mocks God's redemptive plan. After thirty years on the air, "Love of Life" was cancelled with no attempt to end the many plots. Soaps have replaced providence with chance.

The well-known dramas of Samuel Beckett, who wrote such plays as *Waiting for Godot* and *Endgame*, capture the essence of much modern thinking: Humankind is hopelessly trapped by its own make-believe hope in the future, especially its religious faith. Similarly is the soap-opera character caught, except here the theme is far more difficult to discern and the religious implications are not nearly so obvious. It may be that people anticipate an end to soap operas because, created in God's image, they carry in their hearts a sense of beginning and end about themselves and the Creation. The irony is clear: Soaps could not be popular without the existence of God who brought forth the Creation and will see it along to its predestined and full completion. Soaps live off the hope that they offer in anticipation of a happy ending.

THE NEW SERIALS

Soap operas have rarely been used to attract prime-time audiences because of the demands that serialized fiction makes upon viewers. Concerned primarily with maximizing audience size, television executives are leery of programs that require audiences to have a background in the plot or characters. One notable exception, "Peyton Place," was broadcast twice weekly during the prime-time season of 1964–65. Both segments were in Nielsen's Top Twenty, but in the 1965–66 season the telecasts were increased to three times weekly and the ratings declined. Television "series," which revert at the end of each program to the state of affairs among characters that was present at the beginning of the show, are the ideal dramatic form for the profit-minded television industry.

It was therefore a surprise to viewers and critics alike when CBS and NBC started "Dallas" and "Hill Street Blues" respectively. Their success in turn led to the development of shows like "Dynasty," "Knot's Landing," and "St. Elsewhere." Actually, these evening serials are of two distinct varieties. The first type is represented by programs like "Dallas" and "Dynasty," which are *evening soap operas*. The second format, found in "St. Elsewhere" and "Hill Street Blues," is the *ensemble*.

Evening soaps differ from their daytime counterparts in these important respects: faster pace, more action, better acting, more outdoor settings, and more of an emphasis on protagonists. These differences make them more like traditional drama. While some of the characteristics of evening soaps can be attributed to prime-time programs having larger production budgets and being broadcast weekly rather than daily, "Dallas" and "Knot's Landing" create corporate or organizational conflict, something that is less pronounced in daytime soaps. Families and businesses struggle for status and money, wielding collective as well as personal power. Personal trials and tribulations still exist in the evening soaps, but they have become part of a larger battle among self-interested groups. This makes evening soaps more of a single story with all of the subplots related through the development of a major conflict, such as the struggle by oil barons for control of the industry. J.R. is more of a villain than we find in any of the daytime soaps. He is the major source of conflict, and it will not be resolved unless some hero's actions put a stop to J.R.'s tyrannical control of the industry and its individual players.

Much of what has been stated about soap operas also

does not apply well to the ensemble shows. They, too, are episodic, but their characterizations are far more complex and their plots significantly more realistic. Characters display a fuller range of emotions and motivations than do the stick figures of daytime soaps and most other television drama. They learn from past mistakes and are able to change and mature, giving the shows more of a historical and biographical flavor. On "Hill Street Blues," for example, forgiveness is an important, recurrent theme. Ensemble plots are directed toward particularly significant events, and some types of conflict are resolved. Moreover, the ensemble shows tend to deal subtly and provocatively with both personal and collective conflict. Viewers are not so mindlessly treated to unbelievable characters and ridiculous plots.

The ensemble and evening soaps bring to television some new and interesting dramatic possibilities, but they have quickly been converted by the networks into vehicles for exploiting the new audiences. Sex is sometimes depicted gratuitously and excessively. Unnecessary violence is used to spice up weak plots. Characters are changed too readily to satisfy ratings. Overall, what has been an artistic improvement in the more traditional serials has quickly soured. Evening soaps and the ensemble shows may end up as simply two more versions of the struggle for survival.

4

Situation Comedies: Laughing at Ourselves

"The laughter of man is the contentment of God," says Shakespearean scholar Johan Weiss. If so, God must be particularly pleased with American television, since from its earliest days it has elicited chuckles, titters, yowls, and belly laughs. Historian David Marc claims that comedy has always been the dominant ingredient of American commercial television; he calls television America's jester.

But is God really pleased with all laughter? Is laughing at someone who just tripped over a crack in the sidewalk as pleasing to God as a preposterous but enjoyable fishing tale told by Uncle Norman? And what about television situation comedies (sitcoms), especially the more recent versions that rely for their humor on sexual innuendo and snappy put-downs? Is God really content with all of man's laughter?

TYPES OF COMEDY

No one really knows why people laugh. Some say that our laughter is a way of coping with a troubling and fearful world; we laugh to release tension. The German philosopher Nietzsche concluded that man alone suffered so excruciatingly in the world that he was compelled to invent laughter. Others argue that laughter is a response to incongruence; we laugh when we see or hear of two things that don't fit together—the circus clown wearing a pin-striped business suit vest, the bum who quotes Shakespeare, the television news anchor who accidentally swears on the air. Still others believe that laughter is one response to the crude and vulgar; we laugh at people who are less refined or cultured than we.

Actually, humans laugh at many different things and for many different reasons. There are many kinds of humor and comedy. Even comedians disagree about what makes their skits and monologues funny and as a result practice different types of comedy. Rodney Dangerfield pokes fun at his own tragic character who "don't get no respect." Bill Cosby skillfully and affectionately reenacts humorous childhood experiences, remembered in one form or another by all of us. And Don Rickles has made a career out of the insult and put-down. All three comedians elicit laughter, though for different reasons.

The theater has used different types of comedy as well. A "comedy of manners," which is referred to as "high comedy," depicts and satirizes the manners and customs of fashionable society and are meant to be viewed by upper social classes. A "low comedy," on the other hand, uses farce, slapstick, and other horseplay. Early television, groping for large audiences, filled the airways with

variety shows, which were really take-offs of vaudevillian stage. Such low comedies were not necessarily
inferior to the high comedy of the theater but really
reflections of different customs and experiences. Milton
Berle and Ernie Kovacs, two of television's early comic
geniuses, produced some of the most entertaining American comedy of this century.

Students of literature speak of yet another kind of
comedy—the story with a happy ending. Here comedy is
contrasted with tragedy, which is a story with a sad,
usually disastrous ending. This type of comedy may not
move an audience to uproarious laughter but may bring a
smile of joy and hope. Happy endings are enjoyed by all
of us, and television is filled with them.

Over the years many people, including Christians,
have assumed that comedy is inferior to tragedy. Tragedy, they say, is a higher form of art than comedy,
especially compared with the low comedy of farce and
slapstick. Tragedy is serious art, whereas comedy is
merely light and entertaining. Tragedy deals with great
ideas and characters, while comedy wallows in the
mundane and insignificant. This kind of thinking is
simply wrong. Comedy can be a very serious business for
writers, performers, and audiences. Just because we
laugh at a television show does not mean that the show is
trivial. We may be laughing at a character who represents
an important human foible or at an event that reminds us
of something we did that caused other people grief. A
comedy may even address some of the most important
questions that have puzzled mankind, such as the source
of evil and the nature of God. A sitcom like "M*A*S*H"
makes the audience laugh, but it is also at its finest when
it makes people think about war, love, and even the
human condition.

Unfortunately, many Christians have been led to believe that laughter is a sign of human weakness and that the Christian life is a serious business without room for giggles, chuckles, and guffaws. Some Christians even feel guilty when reading a humorous book or viewing a funny program on the tube. Laughter may not always be the best medicine, as *Reader's Digest* suggests, but it is certainly part of our being. All of us laugh, and we laugh at many different things and for a variety of reasons. Part of being human is the ability to see the humor in something and to respond with laughter. Apparently God created us with a sense of humor, so we ought to consider how to use this sense for His glory and honor in our television viewing.

CHRISTIAN LAUGHTER

Laughing itself is the same for believers and nonbelievers. Whether someone follows Jesus should not affect how he laughs. Speaking physiologically, laughter is laughter, given the many types of laughs from guffaws to titters. But what we laugh at, even what we find funny, may change depending on our faith. For the Christian, a particular sitcom may not be funny at all.

As Christians, we should have no problem with the kind of playful humor that all of us experience in our daily lives. A witty remark, an unexpected pun, a humorous recollection—these are daily occurrences that make our lives more enjoyable. Even some of the most serious events, such as business meetings and worship services, are richer and more meaningful when they are open to human laughter. As James Thurber once remarked, "Laughter need not be cut out of anything, since it improves everything. The power that created the poodle, the platypus, and people has an integrated sense of both comedy and tragedy." I recall a church service in which everything seemed to go wrong—the minister announced the wrong hymn number, the front half of the congregation forgot to stand at the appropriate moment, and a dropped offering plate rolled down the center aisle. Still, as we joked about the service afterward, all of us sensed an enhanced spirit of love and community. Our jokes were like a doxology, further praising God for enabling a sinful congregation to worship Him at all!

Christians and non-Christians alike enjoy television because the medium is filled with this playful celebration of our humanness. The sportive remarks and fallible actions of characters such as Bob Newhart and Bill Cosby bring smiles to our faces. And we chuckle over the confusion whipped up among characters in our favorite sitcom, realizing that in some ways our own lives display such confusion. Sitcoms like "Gilligan's Island" and "The Beverly Hillbillies" were based on such lighthearted humor.

For the Christian, however, there is a serious dimension even to the sitcom. Although comedy can be merely play, it can also be serious commentary on our culture and God's creation. Comedy can reinforce our prejudices, fuel our stereotypes, build our pride, and harden our hearts—all in the seemingly benign response of laughter. In this fallen world, laughter, too, is infected with sin.

Christian laughter is ultimately directed toward self. We laugh at characters on the television screen because of what they say about us, about our sinful condition, about our imperfection, about our foibles, even about our silliness. Our laughter is not turned outward as a weapon to make fun of others' assumed inferiority and to build ourselves up, but inward as a barometer of our own pretension and sinfulness. Realizing that laughter can be arrogant, prideful, sneering, vulgar, and contemptuous, we chuckle with humility and compassion.

Satire is acceptable for the Christian only when it does not ridicule others or hold them in contempt. Too often the satire on "The Tonight Show" and "Saturday Night Live" demeans particular public figures, suggesting that an unpopular politician or a show-business personality is a worthless or inferior human being. Comedy of this kind generally elicits scornful laughter by mocking people whose appearance, mannerisms, or ideas we dislike. Often, it encourages an audience to deride others simply because they are different.

Christian comedy recognizes that all people are created in the image of God and that no one deserves scorn or ridicule. Even the most sinful human beings need love and prayers more than hatred and condemnation. Let him who is perfect cast the first stone.

EARLY SITCOMS

Television comedy began with the variety show but quickly turned to the more predictable and profitable sitcom, which has probably been the most successful genre ever created for television. A few of the earliest shows, such as "Ozzie and Harriet" and "Amos 'n' Andy," were simply television versions of popular radio programs. Their success led to the production of dozens of sitcoms written exclusively for the new visual medium. The first hit was "I Love Lucy," a wacky program about a bandleader, his wife, and their frumpy neighbors. Later came "The Andy Griffith Show," "The Real McCoys," "The Beverly Hillbillies," "The Dick Van Dyke

Show," and "My Three Sons." By the mid-sixties, television had given birth to dozens of successful sitcoms, which later went into endless syndication on local stations. Some of the shows, such as "Leave It to Beaver," though not highly rated during their initial run, have nevertheless become part of our popular culture. Practically everyone today knows who the Beaver is, and the original actors have produced a made-for-television movie that updated the characters as they entered middle age.

There was much that was good about the early sitcoms. Most of them portrayed a moral universe that Christians would find unobjectionable—even refreshing—in today's television environment. Early sitcoms generally took place in a stable domestic setting where family members had traditional and definable roles. Fathers usually ruled the nest, although numerous shows suggested that mothers were frequently the backbone of family life. Children on these programs learned the difference between right and wrong and found that wrong behavior would be forgiven in the end. Most of all, sitcom parents loved their children, and it is likely that more than a few American parents learned something of raising children in a positive and forgiving way.

At the same time, however, early sitcoms were almost ridiculously unchangeable. Although Beaver learned a lesson on one show, he would probably have to forget the lesson for the next program in the series. Similarly, parents rarely changed permanently, since they, too, learned their lessons over and over again. One notable exception was "My Three Sons," which matured somewhat over the years with changes among characters and cast. Because each show in an early sitcom series had to revert at the end to the conditions at the beginning of the show, writers were prohibited from making significant changes in setting, plot, and especially character. This gave these programs a simple, predictable quality but made them unrealistic, too.

Many of the more significant social problems during the fifties and sixties were completely ignored in sitcoms. While the shows focused on suburban family life, the urban North and rural South were in the throes of racial upheaval and civil strife. "Amos 'n' Andy," the only black sitcom, portrayed its popular racism in reruns until 1966, when it was finally removed from syndication because of pressure from civil rights groups. Divorce was simply ignored in these series, even though several popular shows depicted the lives of single parents. Worried about program ratings, networks would not allow sensitive issues to be addressed on the air. Consequently, early series depicted a laundered middle-class America, free of the troubles actually plaguing the nation and the family.

Nevertheless, these early sitcoms promoted a very healthy view of humor. Beaver's problems became the audience's problems; we shared in his antics and in his family's love for him. Even the rascal Eddie Haskell was saved from the potentially bitter attacks of a program writer or producer. The audience felt compassion for Eddie in spite of his villainous actions. The laughter of the early sitcom was largely playful and humble.

THE LAUGHTER OF NORMAN LEAR

During the seventies, television writer and producer Norman Lear introduced a number of fundamental changes in the sitcom—changes that influenced the genre into the mid-eighties. Ironically, Lear's most influential show, "All in the Family," was actually an Americanized version of a popular British series, "Till Death Us Do Part," about a middle-class family with a bigoted father and live-in son-in-law. Lear's other hits included "The Jeffersons," "Maude," "One Day at a Time," and "Sanford and Son." While not as controversial as Lear's first sitcom, the later programs relied on a similar formula for their success.

"All in the Family" was the first American sitcom to openly address public issues, including abortion, homosexuality, birth control, and mate swapping. It was also the first to deal frankly with politics, prejudice, and bigotry. Many later sitcoms produced by others relied on Lear's formula, though none were quite as successful. In fact, prime-time television in general was influenced by the popularity of "All in the Family," as evidenced by programs like "Soap." Although not strictly a sitcom, it appealed to the sensational and controversial for its audience.

In one sense Lear liberated the early sitcom from its predictable formula. The old-style comedy, with its simple moral universe and happy endings, was not commercially viable in the turbulent seventies. Americans were not especially interested in viewing shows that peddled certainty in a decade of instability and ambiguity. Simple characters like the Beaver seemed centuries removed from a world where Congress debated whether to impeach the president and America agonized over an ugly and costly war. Lear sensed this incongruity between the fifties' sitcom and the seventies' America and freed the sitcom from the old formula.

Lear improved the sitcom by giving it a sense of

history. Characters were now able to grow and mature, to learn from their mistakes, and to look seriously to the future. Although Archie Bunker remained relatively static over the years, the other characters adapted in various ways to the world around them. Even Archie's liberal son-in-law, Mike, was eventually co-opted by middle-class ideals and sensibilities, consigning himself to the necessity of work by accepting a job as a college teacher. This is not the old-style sitcom, with its individualistic, moralistic programs, but a new genre with the potential for producing worthwhile drama. While Lear does not deserve full credit for inventing this style of comedy—the seeds of it were in a few other shows such as "The Mary Tyler Moore Show" and "My Three Sons"—he should be credited with making it successful.

Unfortunately, Lear eventually exploited the new type of sitcom. First, he opened the sitcom to formerly censored and generally unnecessary language. He was breaking new ground, casting away old taboos to build audience interest and create publicity for his shows. Such language was sometimes a cheap substitute for innovative plots and solid characterizations. Second, Lear chose increasingly sensitive issues to deal with on the shows. Audiences quickly tired of the racial themes, so Lear began switching to sexual topics, such as mate swapping, sexual impotency, and homosexuality. These are important public concerns, but Lear seemed to be less interested in addressing them sensitively and carefully than with using them to build audiences. Third, Lear used some simple, stereotyped characters to further increase the impact of each show. Archie's racist slurs and sexist remarks gave us little insight into racism or sexism. Lear's characters were generally as thin as those of the early sitcoms, though far more evil.

Most importantly, Lear's humor was particularly destructive to the sitcom. A character like Archie can reinforce as well as challenge bigotry and racism. Were we to laugh at Archie because he was such a racist or to see racism in ourselves? Were we to accept Archie, to feel compassion for him, or to condemn him? "All in the Family" and other Learesque sitcoms pointed far too much of the laughter at others and not nearly enough at ourselves. Instead of steering us in the direction of self-examination and contrition, they encouraged us to think highly of ourselves. We laughed at Archie knowing how superior we were, how much freer we were of his bigotry and narrowness. Meanwhile Archie's attitudes and style remained in us, to whatever degree, making us the kinds of sinful creatures who turn our backs on the personal and institutional manifestations of racism in our country and communities. Lear's sitcoms delivered large audiences to advertisers, but it is doubtful that they improved the condition of American society.

PUT-DOWNS AND INNUENDO

During the late seventies and eighties, Lear's brand of comedy lost much of its popularity. One after another, social-issue sitcoms were cancelled by the networks, who replaced them with prime-time soaps, action shows, and the new serials, such as "Hill Street Blues" and "St. Elsewhere." Producers and writers tried to keep the sitcom alive by softening its edges and making it more acceptable for family viewing. The genre relied heavily on put-downs and innuendo to stay alive.

Belittling remarks and crushing retorts have a long history in comedy. Before television, many vaudevillian stand-up comedians and night club performers used such put-downs as a standard part of their acts. Early television variety shows provided new outlets for these comedians, who still found it difficult to make a successful transition from stage to tube. But as the early, moralistic sitcoms replaced the unpredictable variety show, practitioners of the put-down were banished to late-night programs, such as "The Tonight Show" and occasional variety specials.

In the post-Lear era, however, the put-down was reborn. Lear had paved the way with the Bunkers in "All in the Family." The family's arguments about various social issues frequently ended in spirited insults, a far cry from the harmless household discussions of the early sitcom. Archie and Mike verbally attacked each other; Archie and his friends traded salvos; Archie even repeatedly insulted his scatterbrained but well-intentioned wife, Edith. Other sitcoms started using the put-down as a major ingredient; even some of the most family oriented sitcoms used snappy retorts and insults to elicit a few laughs.

For all of its virtues as serious comedy, "M*A*S*H" peddled put-downs probably more than any other show on television. Hawkeye's insults set the tone for "M*A*S*H" the way that moral lessons did in the early sitcoms. In fact, much of the show's popularity may have been a result of its systematic development of antagonisms among the various characters who inhabited the "M*A*S*H" unit during the program's eleven years on prime-time television. The show's characters lived in constant despair and cynicism, expecting each new day at the unit to be just like the last one. New characters came, old ones left, but the tense relationships rarely changed. Put-downs were a way of coping with the seemingly hopeless situation. Perhaps the popularity of the put-down during the late seventies and early eighties was a reflection of the cynicism and despair of the period. Regardless, what made "M*A*S*H" particularly popular during its last few episodes was the growing sense of dignity and respect among members of the unit. Insults were no way to end the series, just as they are no way to conduct one's life. The put-down lost its power as the long-running series drew to a close.

The disturbing thing about the widespread use of put-downs on television is its message about America's own sense of hopelessness and despair. When there is little hope, there is little sense in looking for the good, the beautiful, and the virtuous in life. Snappy retorts draw laughs, but when overused, even on television, they connote disrespect for others. And only in a world without hope is there enough cynicism to sensibly justify disrespect. "M*A*S*H" was perhaps popular not because it accurately captured the spirit of military life, but because it so compellingly captured much of the cynicism of our age.

Innuendo, particularly sexual innuendo, also became a major technique for saving the sitcom in the face of competition from other genres. "Three's Company" was developed specifically because of all the opportunities it afforded for sexual innuendo. Set in Los Angeles, the program followed the antics of a young man who shared an apartment with two young women. The landlord permitted the situation because he assumed the young man was a homosexual. The show was filled with indirect references to various characters' sexuality and to the apparent relationships among the characters. On one level, "Three's Company" and its imitators were simply silly stories about naive characters in confusing and complicated situations. On another level, the program was an excuse for writing and airing off-color jokes and creating sexually oriented humor.

THE COSBY REVIVAL

During the 1984–85 television season, Bill Cosby started a one-man revival of the early style sitcom. When it appeared that even put-downs and sexual innuendo would not save the sitcom on prime-time television, "The Cosby Show" became the biggest hit of the season largely by re-creating the tone and style of the old moralistic comedies. Cosby's series, set in the proverbial sitcom home, affectionately captured the daily experiences of an upper middle-class family. As Cosby said in a newspaper interview, "The viewers like our show because the people in this family really love each other. . . . They know that everybody isn't perfect, but they're trying to help each other."

The success of "The Cosby Show" and some of its many imitations suggests that there was something about the old-style sitcom that will not die—an affectionate look at our own foibles. Instead of insults and jokes directed at others, self-directed humor was the basis for this kind of sitcom. Cosby's plots and characters have prompted viewers to examine themselves, to see the logs in their own eyes, and to accept each other as imperfect beings. His show did an especially fine job of examining parent-child relationships; few viewers would be turned off by Cosby's tender and compassionate portrayals of life in the American home.

Moreover, the Cosby revival of the sitcom was a sign that Americans were coming out of the despair and cynicism of the seventies. These shows displayed a hope and optimism rarely present in sitcoms of the Vietnam era, where only a few shows, such as "Happy Days," with its glorification of an eternal past, conveyed hope for America. The new sitcoms directed the nation's eyes toward a bright future by reinvigorating a centuries-old approach to comedy. Whether the country has a basis for such optimism depends on its people and the Creator of all hope.

COMEDY AND HOPE

The confusion and conflict portrayed in the typical sitcom are funny to us because of the hope we bring to our viewing. We laugh at the ridiculous situations that characters get into because we fully expect that by the end of the show they will have somehow gotten out of their dilemma. Beaver will be reconciled to his father; Hawkeye will rid the "M*A*S*H" unit of an incompetent surgeon who has taken over for the lovable Colonel Potter; Bob Newhart will overcome a writing block prohibiting him from completing the last chapter of a new book.

The best comedy is funny not merely because of clever one-liners or laughable characters, but because of the very structure of a comedic story. As Christopher Fry says, comedy is not an escape from truth, but from despair. If tragedies leave us in despair, if soap operas abandon us in an eternal struggle for survival, comedy at its best suggests that there is hope for mankind. The best sitcoms assert, though sometimes weakly, that human survival is a matter of faith and that things will work out in the end.

But there is a fine line between the healthy laughter of

the Christian and the cynical laughter of the despairing person. For the Christian, laughter is born out of a faith in Christ that all things will indeed work out for good. For the uncommitted, laughter may be merely a response to the absurdity of it all. Comedy can breathe deep the hope that mankind will survive the latest confusion and complication and that reconciliation between God's creatures is indeed possible. Although the gospel is not presented, the Christian is able to fill in the rest of the story. The Christian has that source of hope, that basis for rejecting the laughter of absurdity and despair. Where the sitcom leaves off, the Christian should joyously write the rest of the script: Hope is in the Father, Son, and Holy Spirit—the triune God who reconciled us unto Himself. Knowing that the final victory has already been won, we can laugh loudly.

5

Action Shows:
Visual Fairy Tales

Every decade produces its own successful genre. In the fifties the variety show blossomed under names such as Ed Sullivan, Arthur Godfrey, Jackie Gleason, Red Buttons, and Tennessee Ernie Ford. The next decade belonged to the western, with titles like "Gunsmoke," "Wagon Train," "Raw-hide," "Bonanza," "The Virginian," and "Have Gun, Will Travel." Except for the 1970–71 season, a sitcom topped the ratings for every year of the seventies. What is the genre of the eighties? One possibility is the action show, represented by programs such as "The Dukes of Hazzard," "A-Team," and "Riptide."

On the surface, programs like "Dukes" and "A-Team" seem to have little in common. "Dukes" depicts the harmless antics of southern cousins who repeatedly outsmart the sheriff of Hazzard County. The "A-Team" travels the globe using military weapons and sophisticated machines to combat evil and ensure justice. The plots of both shows are simple and predictable, and the characterizations very weak, which is true of many television programs. While other genres, from sitcoms to westerns, use dialogue to create viewer excitement over their unfolding plots, action shows care little about what the characters say. With a series of visually stimulating scenes—car crashes, chases, shoot-outs—they offer viewers the simplicity of a fairy tale and the visual appeal of an adventure film.

"BATMAN" TO "A-TEAM"

The first action shows to capture large audiences were "Batman" and "The Man from U.N.C.L.E.," both of which made it to the top twenty during the 1965–66 season. "Batman," which appeared twice weekly, was based on the cartoon created by Bob Kane in 1939. Like Superman, Batman held two identities: He was Bruce Wayne, a Gotham City millionaire, and Batman, a masked, caped crusader, who captured crooks by the use of unrealistic weapons and devices. In "The Man from U.N.C.L.E.," two members of an international crime-fighting organization based in New York thwarted the evil efforts of T.H.R.U.S.H. Both programs were semi-comedic adventure stories that made fun of themselves. Rather than creating serious, intense tales of adventure, these shows spun humorous, unrealistic stories that the industry called "camp." "Batman" used unusual camera angles and flashed words such as "Smash!" and "Pow!" on the screen to imitate the comic-book style. "The Man from U.N.C.L.E." was partially a spoof on James Bond stories; the series' executive producer consulted with Bond's creator, Ian Fleming, on the production of the show. Whereas Bond succeeded because of his mental acumen and physical strength, "U.N.C.L.E." characters usually required the aid of an average citizen, frequently a sexy female.

In their own ways, "A-Team" and other action shows of the eighties imitate the camp style popularized decades earlier. Lacking the harsh violence and psychological conflict of early westerns and most cop shows, the genre appeals to young and old viewers alike. Lovable Mr. T and the rest of the quartet smash up vehicles, blow up buildings, and fire rounds of ammunition at the villains, yet rarely is anyone injured, certainly not permanently. Children enjoy the action, and adults chuckle at the ridiculousness of it all.

MILLION-DOLLAR TOYS

Action programs peddle more than heroes and action. They create a billion-dollar demand for program-related toys and paraphernalia. In only two seasons, "Batman" flooded department and toy stores with everything from Batmobiles to Batman and Robin Halloween costumes. Now "Dukes" cars are available in every imaginable size and price category. And Mr. T, the stocky, mohawk-headed character in "A-Team," is depicted in comic books and on lunch boxes.

Action shows are some of the most thoroughly commercialized fare on television. Like television generally, they are made purposely to lure large audiences of consumers to hopeful advertisers. But action programs also sell heroes, role models, and values through merchandising show-related products. Children play "Dukes" games and act out the roles played by the various characters on the show, imitating the antics of program heroes on kitchen floors with their model cars.

Other kids reenact the crime-stopping tactics of the "A-Team" in their backyards, using "official" plastic weapons emblazoned with Mr. T. stickers. Such merchandising extends the life of the television characters into the personal lives of the program viewers. Action shows are television at its commercial best.

MODERN FAIRY TALES

Action shows portray a simple world of easily recognizable good and evil. No currently popular genre so thoroughly and profitably uses uncomplicated and stereotypical characters and events to create a simple struggle between opposing moral forces. Whether it be the automobile antics of "Knight Rider" or the nautical acrobatics of "Riptide," plots are directed toward the elimination of evil. Even young viewers have a sense of who are the good and bad guys, and all viewers know that good must triumph. The central concern in action shows is not determining guilt or innocence, but capturing or frustrating those people already thought to be responsible for the existence of evil.

By portraying good and evil in simple forms, action programs provide American culture with a ritualistic drama of moral conflict. The end of almost all of these shows is predictable: The good characters will be victorious. The genre confirms our belief, indeed our wish, that good will surely triumph over evil. Children, whose moral universe is far less developed than that of their parents, find these simple moral conflicts especially appealing. Except possibly for cartoons, which use many of the techniques of this genre, and educational programs, such as "Mr. Rogers' Neighborhood" and "Sesame Street," action shows are the most popular children's programming on television.

Parents quickly recognize children's insatiable appetite for stories, an appetite that existed long before the advent of television. Even toddlers, not yet seriously interested in the images on a television screen, enjoy hearing stories read from illustrated books. For centuries fairy tales have been the major type of stories for children, and until recent years it could be assumed that most children would be familiar with the popular ones, such as "Snow White" and "Cinderella." But things have changed since the television entered our family rooms and bedrooms. Today young children spend far more time watching television than listening to fairy tales and reading children's literature. Many parents read to their preschoolers, but as the children grow older, such sessions must compete with the visually exciting world of television. In many households television viewing has largely supplanted other forms of storytelling.

The success of action programs is partially due to the genre's popularity with children. Mr. T. and the Dukes are typical of the heroes of American youngsters. Like traditional fairy tales, these programs provide children with imitable heroes, examples of right and wrong behavior, and most of all a sense that good will triumph over evil. Since good and evil are always depicted in simple terms, all but the youngest viewers can participate vicariously in the programs and learn not merely what is right and wrong, but more importantly easily identify with the "right" characters and causes. Each time the "A-Team" thwarts the efforts of a villain, the young viewer celebrates the victory. Action programs are more than children's entertainment; they are potent sources of role models and moral reasoning, especially for children whose parents spend little time with them.

TELEVISION: MANNA FROM HOLLYWOOD?

When parents themselves are unavailable as role models, children turn to others who may not share the family's own moral views or religious beliefs. Perhaps the weakening of the American family was accelerated by the growth of television as the major American pastime.

Psychologist Bruno Bettelheim believes that fairy tales were largely therapeutic for children because they addressed existential issues of importance to all children. He argues that fairy tales have always taught children that severe difficulties are an intrinsic part of human life. Moreover, they have reaffirmed to children that such difficulties can be overcome by steadfast effort even in the midst of unjust hardships. "Little Red Riding Hood," for instance, warns children of the dangers that can be lurking everywhere—even at grandma's house. In "Three Little Pigs," Bettelheim says youngsters learn that diligence and hard work can mean the difference between life and death.

Action shows, on the other hand, make light hearted fun out of death, aging, and human insecurities. They do not explore either the limits of human existence or the wish for eternal life, except in the portrayal of immortal heroes. Visual depictions of helicopter races and squealing tires do little to stimulate the human imagination. Action programs are prettified and simplified fairy tales that subdue their messages and rob them of most deeper meaning.

Moreover, television's version of the fairy tale contains none of the fine language and poetic imagery found in traditional fairy tales and nursery rhymes. Spoken tales and rhymes sensitize young children to the sounds and rhythms of language. Preliterate children may learn to appreciate language and may gain an early interest in reading as the vehicle for entering the enchanting world of words. Comforted by a parent's voice and relaxed by the warmth of the parent's body, children who are read to experience language as love, not simply utility. They may be more inclined than heavy television viewers to make reading and literature part of their lives.

Christians should be especially concerned with the role of action shows in the lives of their children. We, too, wish our children to develop artistic sensibilities at an early age. Language is a gift of God, and we expect our homes to be places where it is used carefully and joyfully. But as Christians, we see that even the most artistically pleasing tale or rhyme tells only part of the story. Our moral universe is predicated on the existence of a loving, faithful God, who redeems and sanctifies His people. God is the source of all good, and evil springs from man's sinful arrogance in the actions of Adam and Eve. Television heroes, however, are far too godlike for our faith; action shows oversimplify the moral troubles of our age. Evil is within us, not merely within the bad guys. So, we raise our children on the stories of the Bible, where the ultimate reference points of good and evil are God and Satan and where human heroes are also Godly servants.

LAUGHING AT VIOLENCE

In the past, parents found it easier to determine if the violence on particular programs was objectionable. Hard-boiled detective shows were off limits to many children; their cold-blooded murders and graphic violence was off limits to many Christian youngsters. Family westerns such as "Bonanza" were often acceptable because of their restraint in depicting violence. Now action shows have confused many parents. Like fairy tales, action shows seem to make light hearted fun of violence. Is such violence totally acceptable? After all, no one takes seriously the antics of Mr. T. Or do they?

On action shows, violence is an attention-getting device. It is not meant to be taken too seriously—after all, we all know the good guys will triumph in the end. Instead violence is to be enjoyed for its visual interest and appreciated for its entertainment value. So we laugh when a semitruck explodes, when a van bounces off a tree and plunges over the edge of a cliff, and when an airplane is turned into vapor. Our laughter is aided because no one ever gets hurt seriously. Bullets, bombs, and bazookas destroy the countryside, but our heroes walk away without a scratch.

On the other hand, action programs trivialize violence. We may remind our children who watch these shows that they are only "make-believe" stories, but this trivializing of violence is not easily understood by young children. Children don't watch television to learn a message, including a message about violence. They're looking for visual stimulation. Once a program meets their requirement of high visual activity, young children are the most undiscriminating viewers. Children under the age of eight are especially unable to make sense out of a story's plot and to understand its theme. They perceive events on the screen but typically don't comprehend how the events relate to one another, what motivates particular characters, and why specific events are necessary for the development and resolution of conflict.

Young children's inability to understand the message and implications behind action programs suggests that parents bear a responsibility to watch and discuss such shows with their children if they permit the kids to watch them. The actions of Mr. T and the other heroes will begin to make sense to young children only as the parents patiently take the time to explain them. Violence is not self-explanatory—not even trivialized violence. Parents might even conclude that there is little redeeming value in some of these programs and that watching them is poor time stewardship.

OF MYTHS AND HEROES

Action programs are predictable and frequently ridiculous stories, but their preoccupation with good and evil suggests that they are important expressions of popular myths. Program after program ends happily with good triumphing over evil. Of course, part of this is due to television's development into "series" drama, where consecutive episodes must begin at the same point where earlier ones began; tragedies are anathema to the series format. But the explanation for the success of these programs runs deeper into the fabric of American culture. Because Americans are a particularly optimistic people, the genre's stories repeatedly conclude on the most optimistic of all notes—good triumphs over evil. This is the theme of many programs—older westerns, police shows—but especially of the newer action shows.

Action programs differ from their optimistic cousins, such as the early television western, in their simplicity of character and conflict. Good triumphed in most westerns, but only after Matt Dillon or Ben Cartwright struggled with the problem of how to combat the evil people, who were making life miserable for the townspeople or the ranchers. Western heroes, like us, coped with their own weaknesses and imperfections, not the silly foible of a Mr. T who is scared of flying. Action show heroes and villains offer viewers none of the rich characterizations and mature conflicts of early westerns and police shows. They are adolescent tales of moral conflict where even the heroes are not permitted to grow up.

Heroes in this genre are powerful and effective. Whether through mental acumen or, more likely, brute force, they accomplish the feats necessary for good to triumph over evil. Some are "superheroes" possessing godlike qualities, but they all offer viewers a godlike salvation from the threat of evil. The Hulk becomes a hero because of his effectiveness against the powers of evil: he dominates other evil characters and confirms the myth that good will be victorious. Providing an obvious contrast with weak characters in soap operas and confused characters in situation comedies, action heroes may be entirely human—even absent minded, fearful, and laughable—but they must be effective at accomplishing good.

Although a number of successful action programs have involved the heroic actions of a team, the genre usually portrays individualistic heroism. Action shows depict the struggle of good and evil in terms of the efforts of individuals, not institutions or organizations. Rarely do these shows suggest that evil exists in institutions and therefore requires institutional change for its elimination. Evil is limited to the intents and actions of individuals, so individual action is the way to solve personal and social problems resulting from evil. As a result, the genre's heroes are not committed to any particular vision of a right and just society but act simply because "it must be done" or because they happen upon a situation that needs correcting. Consequently the specific wrong that they hope to right is rarely tied to any broader frame of reference, moral vision, or religious faith.

The word "humanistic" aptly describes the mythology of action programs. No television genre so clearly reaffirms, week after week, the belief that individual human effort itself will greatly improve the human condition. This genre is evidence of the Fall not only because it portrays evil characters, but more profoundly because it looks to man rather than God for hope. Godlike humans, such as Superman and the Hulk, epitomize humankind's fascination with its own power and ability. Christians must reject this kind of humanistic thinking as well as the universalistic theme of good triumphing over evil for all people. There is a single source of good, the triune God. Evil will not be eliminated by human effort alone, even though God works through earthly vessels. Action programs provide an adolescent sense of security for a culture that groans under the weight of the Fall.

Christians may enjoy viewing programs of this genre, but they are not likely to have their biblical faith increased or their understanding of the human condition enhanced. Moreover, action shows are probably the most artistically inferior drama on television. While most of them are not morally objectionable, neither are they artistically well crafted. They are hardly entertaining beyond the frequent visual antics. Unlike the best fantasy stories, almost all expressions of this genre fail to present a story that gives the viewer any insight into the world where he lives. Action programs are not designed to comment on the day-to-day affairs of people and their institutions, but to reaffirm in visually stimulating ways some of the most basic and popular myths of our time.

THE NEW ACTION SHOWS

Action programs of the early eighties undoubtedly peddled their optimism primarily to young viewers. Most of the shows were broadcast during early evening hours, when preteen children frequently watch their favorite series. Parents watched them, too, although not usually as their first choice, but as the least morally objectionable program for family viewing. The genre's success was always tied to its adolescent themes and young audiences.

With American youth in mind, NBC introduced in the mid-eighties a new style of action show stylistically patterned after the rock videos successfully broadcast on the MTV cable network. The NBC executive who came up with the idea for "Miami Vice" explained his concept to the network's program department in a two-word memo: "MTV Cops." Like its action-show predecessors, "Miami Vice" reformulated the action genre for the teenage and young adult audience, from high-school students to yuppies. NBC added to the genre the latest rock music as well as a visual appeal more seductive than simple car crashes and foot chases.

In "Miami Vice" and its imitators, the actual story means even less than it did in the older action shows. The camera simply follows the whims of the director, capturing whatever picture seems visually stimulating. Women's bodies are prime targets for the camera, as they are on MTV, but beyond such obvious sexual scenes are dozens of unexplainable pictures of landscapes, sky, streets, and buildings. Sometimes the camera even stops for several minutes to show the action of characters who have nothing to do with the plot. The new show relies on predictable story lines and hollow characters—two fashionable detectives who drift in expensive cars and faddish clothes from one ridiculous case to another. Their lifestyles are attractive to young viewers, who purchase the clothing and recordings used on the program.

But "Miami Vice" breaks from its predecessors by adding to the genre's traditional moral lesson—good wins over evil—a celebration of materialism and sensuality. The usually sharp distinctions between good guys and bad guys are eliminated in the show. All that remains are two quasi-hero vice-squad detectives used by the show's writers and directors to capture on film a lot of sensual images and music. The two detectives live the same kind of opulent and self-serving lifestyles as the pimps and drug pushers they pursue. Their narcissistic values are morally righteous only in comparison with the wicked criminality of the drug dealers and vice promoters captured through the detectives' investigations.

If the early action shows were silly and predictable, "Miami Vice" is predictably wicked. By creating visually and aurally pleasing characters, the show hides its wickedness behind a veil of visually stimulating moving pictures, fashionable lifestyles, and expressive contemporary music. The viewer of "Miami Vice" is not watching a traditional detective story, but a series of stylistically connected, carefully crafted images that appeal especially to young Americans caught in the materialistic and narcissistic web of popular culture. As MTV has already discovered, there are many teenagers and young adults who don't care if television tells a story, as long as it stimulates the eye and the ear with pleasing sights and sounds. "Miami Vice" creates a satisfying "feeling" about life for many young people.

TELEVISION: MANNA FROM HOLLYWOOD?

The success of programs such as "Miami Vice" suggests that television now baby-sits young adults as well as it does children. An American toddler raised on "Sesame Street" can move on to the "A-Team," MTV, and finally "Miami Vice," never having to watch visually dull programs. Along the way, of course, he has selected shows that offer less for the mind than for the eye.

STATIC CHARACTERS

Older and newer action shows share a fundamental flaw as children's entertainment: unchanging heroes and villains. Although they frequently display human weaknesses, action heroes always get the bad guys who remain bad guys. The weekly experiences of action characters never motivate them to change. In every program, their personality, their relationships with others, and their view of life remain static. They magically overcome all hardships without ever having to adapt themselves to new situations or to learn from the past. Mr. T and his cohorts will never have to change their ways, since they are always successful. The Dukes will continue outsmarting the law with the same old stunts repeated throughout the country on reruns for years to come. And the "Miami Vice" duo will never have to reconsider their selfish lifestyles.

Children are poorly served by such drama. Far better would be programs that show how characters' experiences help them to mature. Growing up involves learning about the world and adapting to it, something action characters are unable to do even from one show to the next. This is one reason why "Little House" and similar programs were far better for children, who could follow the maturation of youngsters facing personal and family crises. No child can really learn anything significant about growing up from a show that relies entirely on stock characters who remain predictably the same week after week, even season after season.

No matter how severe their difficulties, action characters nearly always catch the bad guys through some ridiculous twist of fate or a simple, instantaneous solution. Like the commercials on these programs, action shows suggest that there is an easy, uncomplicated solution for life's problems. Because action heroes live in the same contemporary world as the child viewer, he is apt to see such heroes as realistic and possible, as the type of hero he should be. These are not the distant heroes of the fairy tale who inhabit a land of make-believe, but are the modern crime fighters, who protect common people from the evil in their neighborhoods and on their streets. Children may become frustrated with their lives when they see that their own troubles are not so easily overcome. They might even start to wonder if they are normal because of their inability to act like their favorite action heroes.

Children need images of growth and development, preferably from parents, siblings, and friends. Action shows alone are no real help to the child looking for maturing role models. It's up to parents to watch action programs with their children, helping them to see how the real world is far different from the one depicted on television. The Christian life offers its own heroes, not the simpleton Mr. T or the narcissistic vice detectives of "Miami Vice," but the faithful and God-fearing keepers of God's covenant promises.

6

Westerns: Civilizing the Savage

America has long loved the West, from the Mississippi to the Pacific Ocean. "Go West, young man, and grow up with the country," wrote newspaperman Horace Greeley in 1850. And thousands of young men took his advice, searching for gold and for that exhilarating feeling derived from the beauty of the land. The West was not simply a place but a state of mind. "Out where the handclasp's a little stronger, out where the smile dwells a little longer, that's where the West begins," said one westerner. "The land of the heart is the land of the West," wrote another.

In the 1980s, the West still beckoned believers. *Vogue* magazine published a *Cowboy Catalogue* to advise young rustlers on the latest western fashion chic. Urban cowboys responded by purchasing $200 eelskin and kangaroo boots, leather vests, and designer jeans. Meanwhile, country balladeer Willie Nelson, whose appearance hardly rivaled that of actor John Travolta in the successful film *Urban Cowboy*, earned a few million dollars inspiring young cowpokes with his electric guitar. "Dallas," a prime-time soap opera about oil barons, became one of the most popular programs of all time. And Barbie and Ken, the famous dolls, got their own horse named "Dallas," thanks to the marketing genius of Mattel, Inc. Even the Christian Broadcasting Network (CBN) went West by resurrecting twenty-year-old reruns of "The Rifleman" and "Wagon Train."

THE WESTERN'S UNIVERSAL APPEAL

Most Americans believe that "the West" and the western are peculiar to the United States, when western styles of life and stories are popular throughout the world. Europe has had a passionate interest in the American frontier for the last two centuries—long before Wyatt Earp and Matt Dillon came on the scene. Since the early 1800s, when James Fenimore Cooper wrote his famous *Leatherstocking Tales*, people throughout the world have read, viewed, and listened to westerns. Scores of authors in Europe alone have produced hundreds of books about the American West, although their popularity says nothing about their historical accuracy.

In Paris, western buffs in Comanche headdresses or sombreros gallop through the Bois de Boulogne—on motor scooters. On the streets of Moscow, young Soviets offer visiting Americans up to several months' pay for a pair of authentic Levi's. Throughout Europe are appearing western fashion shops, specializing in the duds worn by actors on imported American television programs, especially "Dallas." In one of the craziest reports of all, a Scottish health officer complained a number of years ago that the nation's youth were becoming round-shouldered and hollow-chested from imitating the slouching stride of cowboys.

The television western's popularity in other lands was foreshadowed by its tremendous success in the United States. At first it seemed that the genre might cater exclusively to the moralistic instincts of American children. Programs such as "The Lone Ranger" and "Rin Tin Tin," taken from early radio dramas, offered young viewers formulaic tales about righteous heroes, who always brought the bad guys to justice. By the late fifties, however, the success of "Gunsmoke" shifted the focus of the television western to adult concerns. The simple, moralistic shoot-em-up of the kids' western gave way to intense dramatic conflict and moral struggles of the adult western, where rugged cowboys frequently took the law into their own hands. In the 1957–58 season, the top twenty shows included eight westerns, some of which parents judged to be too violent or thematically mature for children's viewing. Among them were the top-rated "Gunsmoke" and the fourth-rated "Have Gun, Will Travel," the story of a professional gunman whose services included courier, bodyguard, and western detective. Another popular show, "Wanted—Dead or Alive," starred Steve McQueen as a bounty hunter who toted an 1892 44/40 center-fire Winchester carbine, which he affectionately called his "Mare's Laig." By the next season, eleven of the top twenty shows were westerns, including the four highest-rated programs.

Although "Gunsmoke" and some of the other adult westerns were successfully distributed outside of the United States, it was the family oriented "Bonanza" that first captured television audiences around the globe. Aired on Sunday evening during most of its popular years, the program became one of the longest-running series on American television. Set in Virginia City, Nevada, it told the story of the Cartwrights, owners of a 600,000-acre ranch called The Ponderosa. Each week the family confronted a specific evil—cattle rustlers, unloving parents, dishonest bankers. By the end of the hour-long program, justice was served and life on the ranch was back to normal. Less violent than many of the earlier westerns and depicting the trials and tribulations of a loving, motherless family, the show appealed to the growing Sunday evening viewing audience of middle-class Americans, as well as the millions of Europeans and even Japanese who watched reruns of the program.

While it's true that only North America was a real-life stage for six-shooters and twenty-gallon hats, the rest of the industrialized world has been just as fascinated with the western as a story. From Cooper's Daniel-Boone-like hero Nathaniel Bumpo to television's Ben Cartwright, western characters and their struggles have taken on universal significance in developed societies. The western is not merely a type of story about America's geographic frontier, but about that universal frontier between human civilization and savagery. People's taste in westerns differ just as do their taste in clothes or automobiles, but at the most basic level the western entertainingly addresses one fundamental question about humankind: Can man be civilized?

WESTERN HEROES AND VILLAINS

Like nearly all popular adventure stories, the television western depicts conflict between characters who represent good and evil. Only in rare instances has the television western portrayed complex characters and ambiguous situations that blur the lines between what is morally good and morally repugnant. Issues of good and bad are almost always clearly distinguished, with an obvious good and an unmistakable evil.

Westerns' moral certainty is obvious in the types of characters found in the typical program. On the one hand we have the good and righteous people, such as the law-enforcing sheriff, the conscientious rancher, the brave cavalryman, and the hard-working cattleman. One of them is usually the hero, although in some of the more interesting westerns they can be the villain as well. Even the Cartwrights on occasion fought zealous fellow ranchers trying to annex distant tracts of The Ponderosa. On the other hand we have the characters who represent evil, such as the Indian, the cattle rustler, the bank robber, and, of course, the proverbial outlaw who commits about every savage crime possible. Although the outlaw is really the perfect western villain because he embodies evil in so many different ways, any type of western character can be depicted as the source of conflict in righteous people's lives.

Between the righteousness of the hero and the wickedness of the bad guys is a third important type of character—the innocent bystander. In westerns set in a typical southwestern frontier town, the bystanders are typically the townspeople who stand on the sidelines as the sheriff and outlaw face off with six-shooters on Main Street. Bystanders are important in other western settings as well. On the wagon train are dozens of innocent families caught in the struggles between the Indians who wish to preserve their sacred lands and the white scouts who make their living leading civilization westward. Railroad and stagecoach passengers also serve as innocent bystanders. These innocent creatures are you and I, the great multitude who watch the show of life as the morally righteous and morally decadent battle all around us.

As anyone who has read historical accounts of the old West knows, the television western, and for that matter most popular westerns in all media, greatly distort the actual conditions and struggles of the frontier. The peace-loving Indians, who were brazenly killed by ambitious and ethnocentric white men and whose food supplies and land were often illegally appropriated, probably are the greatest victims of inaccurate portrayal. Western life as a whole was rarely depicted on television with even the most basic historical sensitivity. The image of the West as a land of violence unrestrained by law is a concoction of the western storyteller, not the historian. Similarly is the clean-clothed, well-mannered western hero largely a product of pen and camera. It's unfortunate that television writers have been so loose in their historical portrayals, for the real history of the West is both interesting and exciting.

The popular western's importance is mythological, not historical. Program heroes, villains, and bystanders are created to build audiences for advertisers, not principally to recount American frontier history. This quest for ratings has created a fictional West that is often highly entertaining but also keeps us from dealing with our nation's actual past. We get on television the West we wish had existed, not the West that Americans really lived. The western hero gives us all hope that good will indeed overcome evil. The western villain reaffirms our hope that evil is not within all of mankind, but within those few people who act depraved and will be held in check by the actions of the righteous heroes. We, as the innocent bystanders, are the concerned citizens who watch the real-life battle between good and evil from the safe distances of the newspaper and the television set.

THE WESTERN AND MODERN SOCIETY

Until recent years, the television western was one of the most popular television genres. Replaced by the situation comedy and the general action program during the seventies, it has made a respectable comeback on CBN, which airs reruns watched by as many as 10 percent of television viewers. Why was the television western so popular in the late fifties and early sixties? And why did its popularity decline so quickly as America entered the Vietnam era?

As mythology, the television western deals with one of the oldest problems facing mankind: the existence of evil in society. Western villains are the embodiment of evil, representing the savage acts of human beings in society. The cattle rustler is an evil character because he does bad things to the righteous—he steals their cattle. Similarly, the bank robber takes the money of people who presumably earned it through hard work and self-sacrifice. The despicable outlaw is evil because he kills and robs innocent people.

The popular western set in the frontier asks and then answers the question: Can human society survive the savage acts of mankind? The question is framed as a struggle on the frontier, where the savage acts of bad guys are contrasted with the civilizing acts of the hero, and where the innocent bystanders hope for the victory of the latter. The frontier is not merely the West in a historical sense, but rather modern society where savage influences are threatening to destroy it.

The popularity of the television western during the fifties and sixties was a hopeful response to the major trends and social-psychological conditions of modern society. Americans wished to believe that society could survive the effects of industrialization: the deterioration of family life, the disappearance of accepted norms of human conduct, and the gradual shrinking of the individual's control over his own life. The appeal of the western is its invitation for the viewer to hope that society will be kept together, that evil will be overcome for all innocent bystanders. The western does not call us to personal change or renewal by telling us that evil comes from within each person and that the future of society rests on individual conversion, religious or otherwise. Instead, the popular western locates the source of evil in particularly savage persons who can be kept in line by the actions of decisive heroes.

Western heroes, from Matt Dillon to Paladin, Wyatt Earp to Bat Masterson, personify the freedom and mastery that no one really has but everyone in modern society would like. They are not like the innocent bystanders, caught up in society's red tape, frustrated over endless schedules and appointments, and fearful about the latest governmental proposals. These heroes are truly masters of their own fate, who calmly solve their problems with a fist and gun. They don't need a family or usually even any close friends. Western heroes rarely marry, since a wife and family would necessitate restraining and confining social ties. They aren't a part of a large organization or bureaucracy. They control their own lives and master the evil world around them. The western portrays a type of person who is, in many respects, diametrically opposed to his contemporary counterpart, a kind of hero most of us wish we were. The genre allows us to participate, psychologically speaking, in a world that is an antidote to the alienated conditions of life in modern society. Through the tube we have great heroic power—or at least we experience such power vicariously.

The western hero is also a man of strong moral conviction, whose goals are so clear that he is able to act always without equivocation. Matt Dillon knows what the problem is and what to do about it. He need not worry about education or ethics. His approach to life's problems is not intellectual or analytical, but intuitive and decisive. For him the issues are clear-cut and obvious: An unmistakable evil must be confronted with the necessary tools of the trade—a six-gun, a horse, and a fist. He uses common sense to its practical extreme—to fight evil.

Such heroes offer the viewer great assurance that the evil in the world can be clearly defined and acted on. Society may be unraveling, the television western asserts, but it can be kept together. Acts of savagery in society can be held in check. I, the viewer, may feel alienated from my family and upset over my hard-driving boss or my unmanageable kids, but mastery of my affairs is indeed possible.

The appeal of the western, then, is not a particularly American phenomenon. This type of program offers hope to anyone experiencing the alienation and savagery of modern society, but people are most likely to believe that society is improving when they are prosperous and relatively content with their own lives. One culture's taste in westerns may differ from another, such as the Japanese appreciation of the teamwork of the Cartwright family, but the theme of the popular western offers hope to all viewers that civilization is possible in spite of man's savagery.

The fifties were particularly optimistic times—economically and socially—in the United States, so it is not surprising that Americans found the western a particularly entertaining form of storytelling. The nation's rapidly increasing spendable income indeed made it appear to the typical American that society was improving.

By the sixties, however, Americans lived in a very different society. Civil-rights conflicts and the war in Vietnam each brought out the savage side of mankind. More than that, these conflicts turned much of the nation sour on the promise of what Lyndon Johnson termed the Great Society. The resulting cynicism in America contradicted the optimistic mythology of the western, and the genre virtually disappeared from prime-time television, although the detective show carried on with its more pessimistic and cynical brand of urban western.

Of course the television writers and producers could have changed the standard formula of the television western. Sensing the mood of the nation, they might have created a new breed of western far less optimistic and more ambiguous in its message. But the competition from the situation comedies was already stiff, and no medium is more faddish than television. "M*A*S*H," "All in the Family," and some other situation comedies captured the cynicism of the period, offering no omnipotent heroes and no simple analyses of the nature of good and evil.

Perhaps the eighties and nineties will together offer a period of relative optimism, where the western will rise once again to its previous televisual glory. Certainly the social problems wrought by industrialization still exist. Any viewing of one of the Christian talk shows would prove that Christians are still concerned about the breakdown of family life and the deterioration of accepted norms of conduct in American society. Maybe this is why CBN's western reruns have done so well in the ratings. It is ironic that the resurgence of American cultural optimism occurred along with the rise to prominence of a new president who hosted one of the few successful western anthology series. The president was Ronald Reagan, and the series was the long-running "Death Valley Days," which made Twenty Mule Team Borax a successful household product.

VIOLENCE AND SIN

It should be of no surprise to the Christian that society sometimes seems to be disintegrating. The western's depiction of "lawlessness" and its portrayal of man's struggle for "law and order" are versions of the real human drama begun with the Fall. Once Adam and Eve partook of the forbidden fruit, it was only a matter of time before Cain or someone else would commit murder, and the savagery of man would be confirmed in deed. The lawless West is one expression of mankind's historic depravity and sinfulness. In the broadest sense, the western addresses not only the savagery of mankind in modern society, but the very sinfulness of mankind's rebellious heart. Do not all people, at all times and places, know something of man's inhumanity to man?

This is not meant to disagree with contemporary sociologists, who point to the savage potential of man in modern mass society. The holocausts in Europe during

World War II and Cambodia in recent years, the growth of terrorism worldwide, and the apartheid policies of some nations all point to man's potential for large-scale savagery. And there is no doubt that the breakdown of traditional sources of authority, including the family, the church, and the community, has escalated the number of brutal acts of violence in modern society. The selfishness and cynicism of middle-class professionals, who commit themselves to little beyond their own career advancement, is one of the marks of the decline of these institutions. As Christians, we must first agree that human beings are, by their fallen nature, rebellious and lawless creatures; we don't need westerns to tell us of our savagery and of the difficulty of maintaining civilization.

Throughout history mankind has created westernlike tales to depict its lawlessness and to reaffirm its hope in a civilized future. The western stories are even analogous to the Trojan tales dealing with the conquest of Asia Minor by the Greeks, preserved in the Homeric poems. Both dealt with the spread of civilization to a new part of the world, the conquest of nature and the natives in that new world, and the slow establishment of law and order after the conquest. Americans today don't like to think of themselves as conquering the Indians, but this is the basis for more than a few highly successful westerns.

The American popular western, however, is a particularly optimistic brand of mythic tale. Its heroes are able to arrest, at least temporarily, the spread of savagery by their decisive acts of violence. "Gunsmoke," the most popular western of all time, retold the myth for 400 hour-long shows and 233 half-hour shows. Beginning with the second season, the program's well-known opening sequence captured the essence of the televised western.

TELEVISION: MANNA FROM HOLLYWOOD?

Matt Dillon and an unidentified badman square off on Main Street in Dodge City. The camera catches close-ups of Matt's face and then of the two holsters as the men prepare to draw their guns. As the guns fire, the camera returns to Dillon's face. The marshal grimaces; he has killed another outlaw. Civilization is saved from the savagery of another depraved individual. The suspenseful gunfight led in many westerns to the necessary, unambiguous, decisive act of the hero—the *sine qua non* of the genre. Once the shot was fired, the program was over; the drama ended. Justice was administered and civilization upheld. The smoke of the gun was the frontier's whack of the judicial gavel—or so the westerns portrayed it.

The western version of hope for mankind points the viewer to heroic experts in physical violence committed to the ideal of law and order. Our hope is in the name of the heroic gunman, brave enough to risk sacrificing himself for the innocent bystanders—us. No society can survive, says the popular western, without heroic acts of bravery and without incurring the costs of violence. None of us would want a society without heroes, but should we embrace the heroic ideal of the western?

First, the western hero may easily present a false hope in our own efforts. Society is held together by the grace of God, not by the self-initiated actions of a few individuals, whether religious leaders or military geniuses. In essence, society is indeed a miracle for which we all should be grateful. Although evil deeds fill the columns of the local newspaper, millions of potentially sinful acts are prevented by the grace of the Creator. Even as civilization grows, human achievements in the sciences, arts, and business make our lives more rewarding;

nevertheless, God indeed deserves our gratitude and obedience for these as well.

Second, western heroism is highly individualistic. The heroes are given almost a godlike status as loners who can accomplish good without the help of others. There are no perfect heroes like Marshal Matt Dillon or rifleman Lucas McCain—who was also the perfect father. Even biblical heroes, from Abraham to Moses and David, had their human weaknesses and sometimes committed grievous sins. Society is held together by the conscientious deeds of people under God's grace, not by the risky act of the great hero. We are all responsible for the moral and cultural fabric of the society in which we live, and the faithful actions of all of us will either improve or destroy the society. Television westerns accurately display the individualistic attitude of Americans, but it is not an attitude that Christians should uncritically adopt. We are all created differently, with various gifts and abilities, but we must learn to work together—Christian and non-Christian—to ensure that our society is just and compassionate.

Third, we must admit that the western's decisive violent acts, such as the shoot-out in Dodge City, are a gross oversimplification of the solution to mankind's savagery. It was ironic that Matt Dillon would reappear each week at the beginning of the program to replay the same shoot-out. Each western show called for its own decisive act until even thousands of shoot-outs had not really eliminated savagery from the frontier, just as none of the battles and murders described in the Bible produced the perfect nation of God-fearing people. There was only one decisive act—Christ's death on the cross at Calvary. Man's own acts have never been decisive, but have always produced further conflict and struggle. Though we taste God's kingdom here on earth, it is only a taste. God's kingdom moves at His pace, not ours, and no number of heroic acts on our part will make His kingdom complete. The history of the world is landscaped with what leaders promised would be decisive violent acts, from Stalinist purges in the emerging Soviet Union to Cambodian genocides in recent years, but none was truly the last. Human hearts always begat more hatred and even greater violence. Many revolutionaries, Marxists, and Facists still falsely preach a gospel of decisive violent action, but violence is no ultimate solution to human sinfulness.

Westerns reassure us of the inevitable victory of good over evil, but they also reflect a suppressed delight in violence for its own sake. We like to see the bad guy "get it," but how much of our enjoyment is with a sense of justice served or with a sense of delight in the violent act itself? If the western regains its popularity, what will be its approach to violence? Will television imitate the Italian "spaghetti westerns" of Clint Eastwood or will it revert to the seemingly benign acts of Marshal Dillon? We should remember that "Gunsmoke" was thought to be highly violent in its day. How our sensitivity to the portrayal of graphic violence has changed!

VIEWING WESTERNS CHRISTIANLY

Western novels, films, radio shows, and television programs have been around for many years, and the recent rebirth of popular interest in them suggests that the genre is more than a fad. While not everyone likes westerns, enough people do to warrant asking seriously whether they may be viewed Christianly.

Let's face it, westerns can be highly entertaining. One of my favorite programs is "Maverick," a twenty-year-old, light hearted series that frequently parodied other serious westerns. Westerns are also engaging; the conflict between outlaws and sheriffs, cattle rustlers and ranchers, can attract and hold a viewer's attention. It's not easy to turn off the television in the middle of an episode of "Wagon Train" or "The Rifleman." Some westerns can even be instructive. The success of "Bonanza" may have been partly a result of the show's moral themes about the family, trust, commitment, and honesty.

But much of what is worthwhile about westerns comes from the way we view the programs, not from the shows themselves. Westerns are stories open to a variety of interpretations and conclusions. When we watch the programs uncritically, we are far less likely to derive any redeeming value from them. We assume they are merely entertainment, when actually they are significant tales of hope, justice, and sometimes even violence.

As stories of hope, westerns contribute along with much popular drama to the widely held belief that human affairs work out for good in the end—a secular Romans 8. Westerns are like the situation comedy, the police drama, and the popular action program because they offer hope to a troubled and confused world. If we see in the western one more sign of God's grace whereby He permits and enables us to make societies and to control the savagery in them, then we add to the program our own Christian interpretation. The programs don't necessarily supply the evidence for this conclusion, but we assume this as a result of our faith. And for the Christian, this is a reasonable, faith-building interpretation. But for the non-Christian the hope offered in westerns need not refer the viewer either to God or to Christ. Instead the western builds and maintains a false sense of security in the heroic actions of men, a naive optimism about the limits of evil in the world, and a sinful ethic of violent justice.

Western justice should also cause the Christian concern. Much of the heroic action we see in the western derives from the motive of revenge. This is personal, not societal justice. It is justice of "getting even," not justice with compassion and especially forgiveness. Our Christian model of justice is God Himself, who might have simply destroyed mankind at many points in biblical history but instead had mercy and compassion, enabling mankind through Christ to receive a special kind of justice. The popular western lacks all but the most superficial compassion, where the hero frees the outlaw after whipping his hide and humiliating him in front of the townspeople. Rarely does the western hero humbly come to grips with his own iniquity. He risks his life to catch the villain, but not out of compassion for the innocent bystanders as much as out of a sense of professional duty.

Watching television westerns Christianly also means that we consider the genre's use of violence. Certainly viewers have different tolerances for graphic representations of violent human acts, but should we really support any program that uses violence simply to maximize ratings and advertising revenues? If the western returns to television, it likely will use violence as a crutch to hold up weak plots, thin characterizations, and silly dialogue. This is the trend in television today, and there is no reason to believe that the western would be immune from it.

7

The Detective:
An Urban Gunslinger

I have never met a private investigator, nor have I known anyone who hired one. Although there are a few detectives listed in the yellow pages, the advertisements say very little about what they actually do. Several ads say "business and personal," which apparently means that they will work for businesses and individuals. A couple of ads also say "surveillance," perhaps referring to sitting in the car at night sipping tepid coffee from a thermos and waiting drowsily for a suspect to leave a sinister-looking apartment building. The ads also list "accident investigation" and "employee honesty" as available services. Nowhere do the yellow pages mention tracking down criminals, discovering dead bodies, or high-speed auto chases. Not surprisingly, none of the local detectives give their picture in the ad, so we don't know if they really wear trench coats and porkpies.

Anyone who has watched television even occasionally

over the last thirty years has an image of the detective. Jim Rockford, Peter Gunn, and Mike Hammer were different styles of detectives, but each contributed to the typical detective stereotype. Detectives are smart but eccentric, driven but relaxed, passionate but unloving. They usually drive a fast car—or at least a slower car extremely well. They carry a gun, usually in a shoulder holster. And if the detective is a private investigator, he often works out of a messy office run by a self-confident, sexy woman who doesn't really need men.

Detective novels and films have been quite successful during the last half-century. We need think only of the writings of Mickey Spillane or the film characterizations of Humphrey Bogart. Loosely defined, many enjoyable mysteries are also detective stories. The adventures of Sherlock Holmes and Lord Peter Whimsey immediately come to mind. But the television detective story has probably contributed the most to Americans' image of the private and police investigator. Think of the names: Cannon, Mannix, Hammer, Diamond, Rockford, Baretta, Magnum, Gunn, Kojak, Columbo. Recall as well the names of programs: "77 Sunset Strip," "Call Surfside 666," "Starsky & Hutch," "Hawaii Five-O," "Vegas," "The Streets of San Francisco," "Barnaby Jones," "Harry O." Television has broadcast nearly a hundred detective programs watched repeatedly by millions of American and foreign viewers. Clearly the detective is one of the great American heroes, even though few of us have never met one.

FROM FRONTIER TO CITY

The detective story on American television is largely an urban western, which portrays the decisive, violent acts of gunslinging heroes struggling to maintain law and order in society. Detective programs shift the focus from the western frontier to the large American city. The enemy is no longer the outlaw or the Indian, but the criminal. The cowboy has traded in Trigger for an automobile and the 45-caliber six-shooter for a snub-nosed 38.

In the western, the frontier typically casts a background of peace and tranquility for the struggles of the cowboy hero. The natural beauty and order of the West contrast with the savage acts of cattle rustlers and bank robbers, creating a hopeful mood for man's ability to maintain a stable society. Man's savage acts are only an aberration, says the western; lawfulness reigns among the animals and across the bucolic frontier. Sheriffs and other heroes are needed simply to squelch the occasional outbursts of human savagery.

In contrast the urban setting gives the detective show a heightened sense of lawlessness. In the city of the typical detective program, the camera rarely catches glimpses of God's beautiful, well-ordered creation. Instead the viewer is treated to frightening and depressing pictures of an urban environment, from dark alleys and deserted shipping docks to cold warehouses and dimly lit night-clubs. Although the city streets may be filled with people during the day, at night they will be deserted and unsafe, speaking of human alienation and warning of impending danger. All of us live in such a world, says the detective show, and there is no ultimate hope, only momentary relief from taking another criminal off the street.

The city in the detective program is the mass society foreshadowed by the popular western. Westerns warned viewers that man's savagery might lead to total lawlessness, and detective shows suggest that society is moving closer to that anarchy. As we step from the western into the urban world of the detective, we experience the bizarre and macabre, from brutal rapes to bloody murders and carefully orchestrated suicides. The western declined in popularity in the sixties, but the detective show held its own, making a prime-time niche even during the eighties. Perhaps the detective program survived because of its more graphic violence and cynical themes. Whereas the western gave us hope in a stable, moral universe, the detective show less optimistically suggests that maybe only violence can overcome violence.

ROMANTIC VIOLENCE

Television detectives inhabit ugly cities but live adventurous lives. Having given up any hope for a completely just society, they have come to enjoy the battle with evil and dangerous people—catching drug traffickers, killing murderers, knocking off hit-men. Detectives hate criminals but love violence, making the detective hero the first major television character to romanticize violence.

The typical detective is a compulsive tough guy who rarely displays any sign of human compassion. His emotions are always under control, even in an apparently helpless situation. He is not scared of death because he deals with it every day; he is cynical about life, believing that the only cause worth championing is violent justice, often in the form of revenge. All personal relationships can lead to unwanted commitments for the detective hero, so he remains a loner, deriving sexual gratification from one-night stands or infrequent rendezvous with a woman "friend" who may even be a client. The detective believes that tenderness and respect weaken him in the urban battle for justice, so he maintains the style and image of the unemotional tough guy.

The hero of this genre is usually a professional gunman. In many westerns the hero was also a rancher, as in "Bonanza," or even a father, as in "The Rifleman." But the detective hero wants no personal responsibilities or entanglements to get in the way of his work. Most television detectives are private investigators or, as they used to say, private eyes. They work for themselves, taking on whatever clients happen to hire their services. Even police detectives are frequently portrayed as eccentric loners, misunderstood by the rest of the department and frequently at odds with the captain or lieutenant. Kojak and Columbo were respected by their peers for their success, not for their lifestyles or mannerisms. Their strange brand of professionalism resonated with the American ideal of the local hero. Both feared and worshiped by society, the detective is a marginal character, outside of the normally accepted standards of behavior, styles of dress, and modes of speech.

Above all, the professional detective on television loves to flirt with potentially deadly situations. His work is a romantic, luring affair with an unknown partner who may try to kill him at any time. His profession is not just work, but a violent, compulsive sexuality. In every episode he courts another unknown criminal, stalking him until justice is done. Eventually in a program's final scene he consummates the increasingly violent relationship with a swipe of the fist or a blast of the gun.

Detective programs celebrate violence strangely. While

the criminals are clearly depicted as the bad guys, it is not so easy to distinguish between the methods used by the detectives and those used by the criminals. Some of the hard-boiled detectives, such as Peter Gunn and Mike Hammer, seem to enjoy violence as much as the criminals. And nearly all television detectives apparently believe that violence itself is a necessary tool of justice. They are not concerned with rehabilitating criminals or even with ensuring fair legal justice, but with punishing evildoers. After all, they say, violent punishment can be an awful lot of fun. In one of the most common detective show formulas, the hero is beaten up by the thugs early in the show. Later, the detective gets his revenge, battering the criminal in the final, climactic scene. Of course the audience enjoys seeing the hero "get even" by administering hand-to-mouth or bullet-to-stomach justice.

This punitive, revengeful attitude would be only lamentable were it not so alarmingly present in the minds of Americans. The television detective actually embodies the widespread belief that people should take the law into their own hands by seeking revenge against those who have offended them or "ripped them off." Several youngsters maliciously scratch the body of a neighbor's new car after he yells at them for running through the flower bed in the backyard. A teacher gives an unfair, low grade after finding out that the student spoke negatively about the course to another teacher. A business executive makes personal long-distance telephone calls on the office phone, reasoning that he is underpaid. The signs of this kind of attitude are everywhere, and certainly the detective hero contributes to it by romanticizing quick and dirty justice. Detectives don't turn the other cheek or examine the log in their own eyes; they are too busy administering their own brand of selfish justice.

By defining crime simply as behavior warranting revenge, the detective show removes criminal action from its moral context. Crime is not merely a wrong against someone, as the shows suggest, but a wrong committed by someone. Criminal acts are sinful deeds flowing from our evil and rebellious hearts. Civil laws, in turn, are gifts from God, enabling human beings to build, maintain, and change society. Of course we may not like all laws in a given society. As Christians, we may even think that a particular law is unjust or morally wrong, but such concern for just and moral laws does not normally give us the personal right to violate laws or to use violence to coerce lawmakers to change them. Then we become criminals ourselves. There may be times when Christians conclude that the gravity of a situation calls for civil disobedience, such as when a government flagrantly violates basic moral teachings, but such cases are exceptions that need not be elaborated here.

Because crime is sin, it will never be eliminated by violent action, no matter how it is romanticized on the tube. Conversion of the individual is the beginning of the solution to crime. Only when hearts are turned to God is an individual likely to respect sincerely the rights of others. Only then is he likely to work with others to change society for the better.

CRIMINAL FACT AND FANTASY

Criminal behavior is a fact of human society, and it would be silly to suggest that television drama ought not to depict any criminal characters or unlawful acts. But our view of what criminality is and our notion of how best to solve the problem of crime are both influenced by popular stories about crime. Similarly, it's doubtful that real detectives take the programs seriously, but it's likely that the public's image of the detective is based on media presentations.

Consider that murder is the most common television crime, whereas in society the most frequently reported crimes are larceny, drunkenness, disorderly conduct, and drug abuse. During prime time, murder accounts for about one-quarter of all crimes depicted; in real life only about one-fifth of 1 percent of all arrests is for murder or nonnegligent manslaughter. In the United States, drunkenness is responsible for more deaths each year than is homicide. According to National Highway Traffic Safety Administration estimates, alcohol is implicated in as many as half of all traffic fatalities, which number about 50,000 each year. Less than 20,000 arrests are made for murder and nonnegligent manslaughter. FBI statistics show that drunk driving accounts for 14 percent of all arrests, more than any other crime. But drunks don't make exciting television characters, and drunken drivers would not make compelling villains, so the networks give us hired killers and Mafia bosses instead of inebriated fathers and intoxicated teenagers. Television emphasizes violent, life-threatening crime, when most crime in society is rather petty and mundane in comparison—a stolen car battery, a questionable tax deduction, fishing without a license.

By sensationalizing crime, television creates a rather narrow view of criminality. We associate crime with professional criminals—people who make their living through murder, extortion, bribery, and the like. Crime is not part of society, but something that a few professionals do to society. We even speak of the "criminal element" as separate from those of us who are "law abiding." Detective shows limit crime to the acts of these few, hard-core toughs who run the criminal "operations." The solution to crime, says the television, is to wipe out these criminals. The detective is then able to legitimize his violent actions on behalf of society. Professional criminals necessitate professional detectives.

Although there are such professional thugs in society, they are not responsible for most crime. Drunk driving and drug abuse, for example, are widespread among middle-class, suburban Americans. So is cheating on federal income tax, dumping household water down city storm sewers, and speeding on the highway. I recall an illegal fund established by a church to enable members to deduct Christian school tuition payments from their federal and state taxes. Many of the more violent criminal acts, such as armed robbery and assault, occur in the most economically depressed areas of urban America. Television dramas almost completely ignore this well-documented link between crime and poverty: People who live in poverty sometimes turn to crime simply to survive. So crime is not only or even primarily the province of the professional lawbreaker, in spite of what television suggests. Laws are broken by all of us, yet we act shocked when a friend is implicated in a major crime.

Detective shows also largely ignore the institutional dimension of crime, which implicates us. If crime is merely the actions of hardened, professional thugs, as the tube suggests, then we are not responsible for it. We might as well cheer on our private eyes who valiantly battle the criminals at their own violent game. But if crime is caused at least in part by the economic and political inequalities of modern society, then all of us who profess to be members of the society are culpable. Much sociological evidence suggests that we are part of the socioeconomic system that produces criminals and fosters crime, and it would be irresponsible of us to wait for Mike Hammer to create a more equitable and just society. He's too busy chasing murderers and women. Surely our society should be better than most at creating economic opportunities for people, but there are vast numbers of minorities and unskilled workers for whom crime and welfare are the only immediate solutions.

If we actually believed that detectives could eliminate crime, we might cite the obvious television evidence: Almost all television criminals are caught. In real life, of course, most crimes go unsolved. Police departments barely have enough staff to respond to citizens' calls and to fill out the necessary reports, let alone catch all the criminals. As any police or private detectives will tell you, they spend very little time actually running after lawbreakers. Television offers hope that the heroic acts of detectives and the police can eradicate crime when, in reality, private investigators themselves are part of a society that promotes crime. Detectives break the law, and not infrequently, trying to accomplish their own brand of personal justice.

There is nothing particularly factual or realistic about the ways that detective shows portray crime and its elimination. Popular drama of this type offers us little more than a mythology of crime, predicated on the violent acts of hardened lawbreakers and the professional violence of romanticized heroes. People in the United States are rightly concerned about crime (a recent study found that two of every five Americans are highly fearful that they will become victims of violent crimes), but there is no reason to believe that detective shows will improve the situation.

SAVING US FROM CRIME

As the media-appointed antidote to crime, the detective saves us from savage hoodlums and other lawbreakers. We are the innocent bystanders, the nondescript people who walk the urban streets during the day. He is our hope and our salvation, to describe him in religious terms. But why the detective? Why is it that the lone private investigator, instead of the police department and the courts, is frequently the source of our salvation from crime?

The evolution of detective programs over the years says much about America's declining faith in traditional law-enforcement institutions. Many early shows such as "Dragnet" portrayed the police detective as an effective crime fighter and defender of justice. Even the early private investigators frequently collaborated with the police and other government agencies. But today "Dragnet" and the others seem stilted and moralistic, and adult viewers prefer the morally uncertain characterizations of a show such as "Hill Street Blues." Although the newer detective programs are different in many respects, and certainly more realistic, they share with nearly all adult-oriented, contemporary police programs a morally ambiguous view of traditional law enforcement.

Police are typically portrayed today in adult television drama as inefficient, incompetent, and often even corrupt—a far cry from the upright character of Sergeant Friday. By today's viewing standards and social mores, Friday is a wimpy organizational man who always plays by the rules. It's hard to believe that "Dragnet" was once serious adult drama; many people now watch it as an entertaining look at how silly television used to be.

Certainly the newer shows are more realistic, as anyone who reads the newspaper would know. Especially in urban areas, there are incompetent and corrupt police who are more concerned with their own professional advancement or financial gain than with serving the public. And law enforcement does frequently create the kinds of psychological and emotional stress depicted on "Hill Street Blues." No doubt some detectives do sleep with their clients, as happens on "Miami Vice." In comparison, the Sergeant Fridays of the past were indeed stilted.

But it's no longer easy to distinguish between the good guys and the bad guys. "Miami Vice" detectives drive the cars and wear the clothes formerly owned by wealthy drug traffickers; police and criminals seem to share the same materialistic and narcissistic values. On "Hill Street Blues," the personal and professional lives of police are so intertwined that it's difficult for the viewer to distinguish between the police and citizens or between the police and criminals. Police are crooks, too— and not just an individual bad egg, but nearly entire departments. By emphasizing the fallibility of police officers and detectives, a show such as "Hill Street Blues" significantly alters the message of the genre.

Television programs increasingly express a deep uncertainty about the ability of traditional law-enforcement agencies to ensure personal security for citizens and to promote justice. They seem far more optimistic about the heroic actions of the individual detective, particularly the private eye. The detective has become one of the great heroes of American pragmatism, liked because of his ability to get the job done. His personal morality and intellectual virtuosity are unimportant when compared with his crime-fighting accomplishments. He does what the police are often unable to do because of their departmental bureaucracy, personal fears, or lack of imagination. Even luck is frequently on his side. The television detective may not always know what he's doing, but his tenacity, luck, and physical force will ultimately triumph. He'll get the criminal.

Detective programs significantly portray the detective as above and beyond the law. He necessarily breaks the law on occasion to ensure justice. In hundreds of shows the detective has assumed illegal aliases, beaten up criminals to get them to "talk," paid off informants, and violated the basic rights of suspects. He uses violence, treachery, and corruption to battle evildoers, taking the law into his own hands.

The contemporary detective program is evidence of the nation's decreasing faith in the ability of established institutions to fight crime and ensure justice. Perhaps these shows are popular because Americans actually believe that law enforcement agencies are unable to control crime. In recent years some Americans have made heroes out of frustrated citizens who took the law into their hands in subways and on city streets. Life in the city is looking more and more like the savage world portrayed on the detective show.

CRIME AND COMMUNITY

The modern American city is not only the center of crime and corruption but also the home of concert halls, art museums, theaters, and magnificent architecture. A city such as New York, which has been the setting for innumerable detective programs, is sprinkled with some of the world's finest cultural achievements. But of course, the streets of New York are indeed dangerous, and the cities of this land are fertile beds for the growth of criminal activities, from the work of the Mafia to the petty crimes of schoolboys. There is always a sense in the modern city that "it is the best of times and the worst of times," to steal a phrase from Dickens.

If we think of the city as a metaphor for the human condition, we conclude that God's grace and mankind's rebelliousness coexist in all human activities and societies. Some of what we do seems to be beautifully in harmony with God's laws but out of place in the fallen world—like an attractive art museum in the middle of a street littered with decaying garbage and lined with gutted apartment buildings. Other times our words and deeds create disharmony in our own lives and in the lives of those around us.

In the broadest sense the genre captures accurately the human condition: We do live in a savage world like that traversed by the private investigator. Our fears about our own safety and about the future of society are exploited by the writers and producers who create the detective's environment. But what is the source of the detective's hope? Is there really any basis for our hope that savagery will not engulf the city, as it once did the earth before the great flood?

Into the fallen urban world of the detective program

steps the heroic private investigator, offering us a misplaced hope in the city's own regenerative powers. He gets the criminals, and we get the idea that things will improve when we begin taking the law into our own hands. Violence may not pay for the bad guys, but it sure pays for the private eye. We simply need to work diligently, take advantage of luck, intimidate others when necessary, and the world will be a better place to live in. The detective is not only our hero, but our map for how to get to the just society we all wish to inhabit.

Although the arrogance of the detective is clear, we will not create a just society by heeding his advice. His hope is in himself; ours is in the name of the Lord. He beguiles and intimidates; we love and serve. He is a loner; we are part of a community that lives and works together.

Humanly speaking, our best antidote to all types of crime is to strengthen the communities where we live. When we live in harmony, watch out for each other, respect each other, and provide for each other, crime is greatly reduced. When we have no idea who lives next door and our major concern is building fortresses to protect our riches, our communities will turn into the cold, scary places depicted in the detective programs. The detective has little or no respect for traditional institutions, including the family, the community, and the church. He has consigned himself to living like the very people whom he battles—criminals alienated from each other and the communities where they live. Consequently he lives in cynicism and despair.

For us there is no reason for such despair. There is hope beyond catching bad guys and intimidating thugs. In community we can share in that hope and build the kind of world that brings the hope to all mankind.

8

Rock Video: Dancing to Despair

In the fifties it was Elvis Presley, the hip-thrusting southerner who sang "Jailhouse Rock" and "Heartbreak Hotel." The sixties brought us the Beatles, whose British accents and moplike locks gained the attention of youth throughout the world. Rock music produced dozens of stars during the turbulent seventies, but none that rivaled Presley or the Beatles. And then came Michael Jackson. As a member of the Jackson Five during the seventies, he attained moderate fame and substantial wealth. After the release in late 1983 of "Thriller," a combination rock album and video, Jackson became rock's greatest star. The album sold over 36 million copies during the first seven months, making it the best-selling record of all time. Jackson's subsequent concert tour led to the kinds of long ticket lines and frenzied audiences characteristic of earlier superstars. Jackson was the first major rock star packaged and promoted visually through the new popular art form called "rock video."

EVOLUTION OF ROCK 'N' ROLL

As strange as it seems today, there was no "rock 'n' roll" before World War II. During the war years many blacks moved from the rural South to the northern industrial centers in hopes of finding employment. They brought with them their taste for "country blues," which was urbanized by the inclusion of a heavy beat or rhythm. Black radio stations began playing this new "rhythm and blues," eventually capturing many white teenager listeners. Meanwhile country singers, such as Billy Haley ("Rock Around the Clock"), combined their music with rhythm and blues, producing a style known as "rockabilly." After the war hundreds of small, independent recording studios and record companies signed white country singers to make rockabilly for white teens. Elvis Presley was one of the first singers signed by a small company. He later signed with RCA, who promoted his music and created the world's first major rock star. From the beginning, rock has been a combination of art and hype.

Radio stations across the country cashed in on the rising popularity of rock music by playing the new records twenty-four hours a day. On many stations rhythm and blues, country, and other types of music were replaced with "Top 40." Young listeners heard a new kind of radio—repeated station identification, hard-sell commercials, sound effects, fast-talking disc jockeys, and record promotions.

Record companies and radio stations together packaged rock stars and promoted their records, concerts, and other public appearances. A few major recording companies and radio stations resisted rock 'n' roll for a variety of reasons: uncertainties about the long-term future of the new music; pressure from religious organizations against sexually explicit lyrics and sexually implicit dancing, such as Presley's pelvic thrusts, which were not shown when he first appeared on "The Ed Sullivan Show"; and public sentiment against "Negro" music. But the national popularity in 1956 of Dick Clark's television program "American Bandstand" signaled the social acceptability of the new music. The predecessor of rock video programs, "American Bandstand" remained essentially the same in the eighties as it was during the early years— dancing, guest appearances by rock stars, and record reviews. Through the commercial efforts of radio stations and programs like "American Bandstand," rock music became the major form of entertainment for young people. By the mid-eighties, popular music accounted for about 85–90 percent of all record sales, and 75 percent of the sales were to twelve- to twenty-year-olds.

Since the early popularity of rockabilly, rock 'n' roll has seen many styles. Even individual groups such as the Beatles changed their music significantly over the period of their popularity. There is hard rock, acid rock, country rock, soft rock, punk rock, new wave, and heavy metal. There is also so-called Christian rock, which varies tremendously in musical style and even lyrical content. Some of its lyrics are God-centered sections from Scripture; others are stories of conversion or religious experiences. Rock music is like teenage fashion: There are numerous styles and tastes, changing with shifts in American culture. It is not possible to predict with accuracy what types of rock music will be popular in the future, and this makes the recording business a highly uncertain and speculative industry.

ENTER MTV

The beginning of rock video is usually associated with the establishment in 1981 of MTV (Music Television), a cable television channel devoted to rock music twenty-four hours a day. It came along at precisely the right time. Record sales were declining, and industry executives were ready to try just about any new promotional gimmick to stimulate the industry. Radio wasn't creating a hungry class of rock record consumers, and concert tours were too expensive and time consuming. A few record companies believed MTV was the answer to the industry's financial woes.

MTV is a visual version of the Top-40 radio station, playing short videotapes instead of records. These videotapes—or "videos"—are introduced by MTV's own VJs (the equivalent of the DJ), who also pass along to viewers the latest gossip about rock stars and disseminate information about concert tours. Television commercials also gave MTV the sound of rock radio stations. By the mid-eighties MTV was available to about 20 million American viewers, and plans were underway to establish similar channels in Europe. MTV turned a profit in 1984, charging local cable companies ten to fifteen cents per subscriber. Television stations and the networks began their own rock video programs as well. Of all of the cable networks, however, MTV achieved the fastest success.

Videos are free commercials for rock groups and record companies, both of whom make money from record sales, and MTV sells records. The phenomenal popularity of Michael Jackson is attributed, in part, to MTV. He was the first rock star for whom a record company spent over a million dollars to produce several filmlike

117

videos—"Beat It" and "Thriller." Worth the expense, sales of the "Thriller" album tripled to $600,000 per week within a week after the video appeared on TV. Some successful rock groups, such as England's Duran Duran, were virtually unknown to American audiences until their videos began playing on MTV. Because of the influence of MTV, some groups' records began selling even before they were aired on radio stations. Sixty-three percent of viewers say that MTV influences which records they buy. One study found that MTV viewers buy an average of nine albums a year and about half of their purchases are influenced by what they see on the video channel.

Record companies are now signing particular rock groups because of their visual appeal and less because of their music. Rock lyricists, in turn, write songs based on particular visual ideas that they believe will make good videos. The success of MTV proves that television today can generate among teens more interest in popular records than radio can. In a society dominated by the medium of television, radio is too unspectacular for most record promoters, who like television's visual ability to hold an audience's attention and create a visually stimulating environment that keeps the viewer's mind suspended in the constant flow of images. According to its creators, the channel communicates mood and emotion; viewers are not expected or encouraged to think, but to feel. VJ studios simulate a bedroom or loft—a place where the individual viewer and the VJ together watch the videos. Although the VJ segments on MTV are taped in advance, misstatements and other mistakes are often used on the air to further enhance the spontaneous, live effect. Lighting in the studios is low and dispersed to avoid a bright, television-studio appearance. The strategy works: The channel received almost 100,000 letters per month during the first year, and many viewers wrote to individual VJs.

STYLES OF VIDEO

It is the videos themselves, however, that show how MTV sells records. There are four types of rock videos. Each one uses particular types of visual imagery to create the desired effect.

1. The Performance Video

Performance videos are tapes of a live or staged performance by rock groups who have performed on mountaintops, in a foggy meadow at sunrise, in the desert, and on the streets of an urban slum. Most performance videos are staged for the cameras, not for an audience, so producers and directors can create a more effective visual presentation. Actually, the success of many performance videos has shown how unimportant it is that it be staged realistically. Frequently microphones and electric guitars are used without wires, amplifiers, or even speakers. In some cases, the timing of the music in the audio portion of the video does not match the timing of the staged performance. The strangest concert videos show the rock group's members performing with no instruments or electronic instruments present, often out-of-doors or in a studio carefully created for its odd or stunning visuals.

2. The Story Video

Folk musicians have always told stories through ballads, and a few rock lyricists have carried on the

119

tradition. Harry Chapin and Jim Croce, both of whom died tragically in the seventies, are best known for their musical storytelling. Now video producers create visual ballads by translating a rock song's lyrics into a video narrative. Sometimes the vignette is obviously related to the song's lyrics; more often the visual narrative is unrelated to the song.

In the song "Gimme All Your Lovin'," the group ZZ Top sings about sexual love, apparently between a man and a woman. The video of the same song narrates a story about a young gas station mechanic who gets picked up by a carload of women dressed as prostitutes. They take him overnight to an isolated spot in the country and dump him from their car at the station the next morning. Meanwhile, the crotchety owner of the service station is carefully examining the glossy pages of a girlie magazine while rocking in a chair. The scenes in the video were chosen for their impact, not for their relationship to the lyrics or music. The song's lyrics say nothing about gas stations, prostitutes, group sex, or girlie magazines. Video artist Tim Newman, who produced the video for Warner Brothers, said, "Basically, the theme of the video is just male-adolescent fantasy; the message of it is, these girls may come into your town next."

3. The Dance Video

Rock 'n' roll has always been dance music. Its simple, potent rhythms naturally move the mind and body to clapping, swaying, shuffling, and the like. So it's not surprising that some videos simply capture people dancing to the music of rock groups. Occasionally members of a band or a solo singer will dance alone. Usually the group will be joined by other skilled dancers.

The movements of skilled dancers along with the shots of well-known rock musicians elicit strong visual interest among video viewers. Apparently dance videos don't hold viewer interest over repeated showings, however, leading many producers to combine this type with other kinds of videos.

4. The Abstract Video

Abstract videos contain rapidly changing visual images with no logical or symbolic relationship to each other, much like scenes in the theater of the absurd. They are simply a disjointed series of visually exciting images pieced together to fit loosely with a song's lyrics. Most abstract videos depend upon bizarre or eerie shots— slow-motion doves flying through a castle lit with candles; hundreds of teenagers dressed in armbands and giving Nazi salutes to a rock group. Abstract videos typically use sex and violence, but the overall theme of most of them is unclear. Says one video director, "Directors take these songs by groups who have nothing to say and try to contrive a handle by repeatedly using an object and implying that it is some kind of totem. The number of girls on MTV picking up wine glasses and lockets and earrings and breaking them or stepping on them with high heels cannot be believed."

One of the major abstract video producers, Russell Mulcahy, describes his work this way: "I just put myself in the position of the audience and try to please myself. . . . I just think, 'Do I want to be uplifted here, or mystified, or tantalized, or what?' Usually I come up with one image, one impression, and base everything else around that."

COMMERCIALS FOR MEDIA BABIES

MTV and the other rock video programs are tuned to the media generation. Raised on the tube, many of today's teens and young adults are attached to television and radio, as if the media were umbilical cords. Radio and television are an important part of their lives, and young people's nervous systems have adjusted to the nearly constant barrage of aural and visual stimulants. Some young people find it difficult to study without noise from a radio; others carry radios with them all day long. Now MTV with its visual merry-go-round offers young viewers a ride every hour of every day.

Almost all videos share one major characteristic: a frenetic pace. Even dance and story videos pack dozens of different images into every minute of television time. Viewers are bounced from camera-to-camera and scene-to-scene to prevent boredom or inattentive viewing. In this respect videos are more like commercials than dramatic programs. Every second of valuable air time is used to manipulate viewers. There is no place for viewer reflection, no time for thoughtful analysis or evaluation. Video producers have only four or five minutes to gain viewers' attention, create a mood, and leave them with the desire to buy the record. Video after video jumps across the screen with breaks only for advertisements and comments from VJs.

Videos are styled after television commercials. They are conceived and produced by technical wizards many of whom formerly made their living creating advertisements. The frenetic pace, the rapidly changing images, the shifting camera angles, the carefully synchronized music have long been used by the advertising industry to capture viewers in half-minute commercials. One study found that rock videos are punctuated by extremely rapid shot changes, averaging twenty shots per minute. Only television commercials, which are packaged in half-minute periods, have a more frenetic visual pace. Some advertisements on television are hard-sell appeals, but most are, like videos, visually powerful vignettes. The Pepsi generation is a mood or feeling created in the commercials. Now the Pepsi generation has its own television channel creating moods all day long—MTV. Even popular network television commercials are now stylized after rock videos. Beer and automobile advertisements increasingly resemble videos. Television commercials and rock videos are kindred spirits.

The flickering images of rock videos parallel the nervous anxiety of our contemporary youth. MTV creates a nerve-racking ambience that fuels the sensory needs of a generation raised on television. Patience and delayed rewards are lost virtues. MTV executives chose "I want my MTV," a take-off from the old "I want my Maypo" commercial, as a slogan for the new channel. It was to be a television channel for the new generation of video babies. As one of the founders of MTV puts it, "Our core audience is the television babies who grew up on TV and rock and roll. . . . The strongest appeal you can make [to these TV and rock babies] is emotionally. If you can get their emotions going, [make them] forget their logic, you've got 'em." Short attention spans, poor writing abilities, and general boredom are attributed to many factors, but most educators agree that television is at least one of the culprits. Rock video is a further extension of television into the lives of America's youth, and it is likely that young people will suffer the results, while the music industry reaps the profits.

TELEVISION: MANNA FROM HOLLYWOOD?

Rock videos have shifted power in the music industry further into the hands of the promoters. Elvis Presley and the Beatles were the victims of record promoters in their day, but these early groups could choose the image their music projected. Their records still contained their own raw material—lyrics, melodies, title. Videos, in contrast, are almost completely in the hands of video producers and directors. These marketing professionals typically write, shoot, and edit the videos, determining what the viewer sees and what mood is created. They package the music as a visual commercial. As the rock-music journal *Rolling Stone* concluded, "MTV's most stunning achievement has been in domesticating the relatively media-primitive field of rock and in coaxing it into the ultracommercial video arena, where products lose identity as anything but products, where it is impossible to distinguish between entertainment and sales pitch. . . . It's tough to avoid the conclusion that rock and roll has been replaced by commercials."

HIDDEN MESSAGES

It's possible that videos convey hidden meanings. Some people believe that many videos subliminally communicate satanic and evil messages. Abstract videos do portray strange and eerie images of semihuman characters, such as a flying choirboy backed by a chorus of teens with lighted eyes. And a few rock groups have undoubtedly used satanic lyrics and visual symbols in their music and at their concerts. But most videos, like most rock music, are not meant to communicate any particular religious or spiritual ideas. Videos instead emphasize sexuality, mobility, and other things of interest to young people. Moreover, there are hundreds of rock groups and video producers, whose religious and theological backgrounds vary from evangelical to agnostic and atheist. It is unlikely that rock music generally or videos specifically are part of a satanic conspiracy to claim the souls of teens.

Most abstract videos are better explained as the gimmickry of promoters, visually attuned to the interests and preoccupations of teens and young adults. Whatever happens to be in style—fashions, dances, cars—is bound to appear in the latest abstract video. And the strangest or most bizarre shots are simply someone's wild notion as to what will catch viewers' attention and hold their interest. Unfortunately, many teens believe there to be some great significance behind each of the scenes in an abstract video, and they watch them repeatedly, hoping that eventually the meaning of the video will become clear. Most videos are meant to create little more than a visually induced feeling or mood, and attempts to figure them out can be very frustrating. Although abstract videos do give the impression that they contain some great message, most of the time they are simply absurd.

If videos are not directly satanic or occult, what is their message? What is the mood of the videos? What feelings do they arouse? Though there are exceptions, videos project a world of despair. Video characters inhabit a depressing, fatalistic world, largely devoid of love and tenderness. People find only momentary happiness in the fleeting sensations resulting from sex.

VIDEO SEX

On videos, sex is the most frequent route to a meaningful life. Approximately three-quarters of all videos played on MTV involve sexual relations, usually between a male and female. Story videos portray various sexual acts between unidentified couples or between rock stars and other characters. Dance videos show sexually suggestive movements of people in various states of dress. Abstract videos depict sexual relations often in obscure or highly symbolic images, such as fires, cigarettes, microphones, and balloons. Videos even portray teen sexual fantasies, including relations with middle-aged members of the opposite sex and with teachers.

Video sexuality is usually selfish, violent, and without love. Most rock videos erroneously suggest that a person should seek such sexual relations. Some videos even link violence with sex. Sadism is a frequent theme in performance and abstract videos. Males are portrayed as powerful animals, inflicting sexually arousing pain on their female partners. Chains, belts, and whips are used or simply displayed. Rarely are sexual relations depicted with tenderness and respect. Video sex is aggressive. Sex is what someone gets from someone else; sexual relations are taken, not given. Young people who watch MTV and other video programs are fed childish and immature views of human sexuality.

Of course, human sexuality is not meant to be evil. God created us, male and female, as sexual beings. Teens are naturally curious about their own sexuality, and they turn to rock videos to find out about it. Like advertising and teen films, rock videos glamorize distorted views of sexuality and sexual happiness. The answer to MTV is not to condemn sex or criticize the media, but to create in the home the type of environment where human sexuality can be discussed openly by parents and children. We have to provide biblical answers for teens' questions, and we must do it lovingly and sincerely. If parents don't establish a Christian understanding of sexuality in the home, the media's sinful sexual ideals will look most attractive to curious young people.

Along with sex, video characters look to music and dance as routes to happiness. Many videos are filled with talented dancers and their artistry, but dancing itself is almost invariably the source of characters' enjoyment. There is no apparent reason to dance other than that it "feels good." Rock rhythms sometimes bring smiles of delight to video characters, but the implication is that despair sets in when the music stops. Happiness is the temporary euphoria induced by rock 'n' roll.

VIDEO DESPAIR

One could watch MTV for hours without seeing any clear signs that there is truly any hope for humankind or beauty in God's creation. Death, destruction, and cynicism blot out all but the temporary, self-indulgent joy derived from sex and music. Rock stars and actors are set in a world where selfishness is a virtue and sexual pleasure the primary end in life. Absent are signs of God's grace, self-sacrificing love, human warmth, compassion, and community. These are out of place in the kingdom of video, where despair dominates MTV.

Rock videos capture the peculiar sentiments of a generation born in social and personal alienation. Many young people today feel the kind of restlessness and cynicism projected in these videos, and it would be naive for us to dismiss MTV and its imitators as the artwork of a small group of drug-crazed hippies or satanic cultists. Much of contemporary rock music is the outgrowth of post-Modernist thought, which emphasizes immediacy, uncertainty, and the feeling that nothing really matters.

Videos reflect and reinforce this view of life, and traditional institutions—such as the family and the church—have done little to stem the tide. Christian writer Lloyd Billingsley rightly calls MTV's audience a "goose-stepping *Konsumerjugend* with disposable income, living under a dictatorship of freedom, and waiting to be told what to do and buy."

There are those musicians and performers who are trying to redeem rock music. Names like Donna Summer and Cliff Richard are frequently invoked by optimistic believers who hope that stories about these stars' conversions are accurate. Then, there is the increasing number of Christian groups, whose lyrics deal explicitly with religious themes. Finally, there are even a few groups, most notably U2, that have entered the video market with their rock music and Christian messages.

While the impact of these and other Christians on rock music and the record industry has been largely insignificant, we should be reminded by their efforts that rock music is not inherently evil or demonic. Musical enjoyment is, by and large, a matter of taste, and there are artistically superior and inferior examples of all styles of music. Rock may not be appropriate for Sunday morning worship services in Middle America, but in other cultures, such as those of Nigeria, strong and rapid rhythms are an important part of the musical tradition. Unfortunately, some Christian groups simply imitate the video techniques popularized by the industry and make no attempt to create distinctive videos that better respect the audience. A video by one Christian group was even rejected for air play on MTV because of its violent depiction of the Antichrist being engulfed in flames.

In the United States, however, rock music is foremost a

business. MTV is the product of shrewd entrepreneurs who know how to package and promote people. As a result, rock music and videos are the creation of an industry governed largely by the love of money. Individual Christian rock musicians stand little chance of greatly improving the rock-video industry, let alone the major recording studios. Many hearts would have to be softened and souls converted before the American rock establishment would take seriously Christian concerns about rock videos.

Most Christian groups fail to create artistically superior music. They expect the religious lyrics themselves to make their songs superior to "non-Christian" songs, while ignoring musical standards. Sadly, most so-called Christian songs played on radio are little better than elevator music, and MTV will probably make matters worse. Videos stress images, not music. Record sales are increasingly contingent upon visual gimmickry, not musical artistry. Christians who want to make videos will have to grapple with this dilemma.

Rock's history suggests little hope for change. Born of rhythm and blues and working-class experience, rockabilly was transformed by the record promoters and talent agents into rock 'n' roll. From there rock became the major entertainment for middle-class kids from relatively affluent backgrounds. It sang of personal despair but also offered visions of romantic and material happiness. Soon the fun of beach parties and sockhops was replaced with the cynicism and selfishness that have come to characterize rock video in the eighties.

Perhaps Michael Jackson's success stemmed from the upbeat mood of his music and the carefree spirit of the break dancing that he popularized. His music represented fleeting happiness for many young people looking for joy in a broken and confusing world. It gave our youth something and someone in whom to believe temporarily. Sadly, Jackson's version of happiness is whipped up by the promoters who stand to gain by Michael's stardom.

Rock music can only be redeemed in the context of Christian community, and it is precisely this community that either dogmatically rejects it or uncritically accepts it. Currently rock is the music of a confused and alienated youth culture badly in need of the warmth and fellowship of the church of Jesus Christ. MTV accepts this culture and seeks to use it for its own commercial ends. Whether Christians turn their backs on rock music and MTV, they cannot reject the people for whom rock is both a weak source of comfort and a prelude to further despair.

9

Television and the Church

All of us complain about television occasionally. Sometimes we echo the complaint of comedian Ernie Kovacs about the poor quality of television shows, "Television—a medium. So called because it is neither rare nor well-done." Other times we decry with Orson Welles as he speaks of television's addictive power, "I hate television, I hate it as much as peanuts. But I can't stop eating peanuts." And we all have shared British critic Clive Barnes' fears about what people like to watch, "Television is the first truly democratic culture—the first culture available to everybody and entirely governed by what the people want. The most terrifying thing is what the people do want." For the Christian, there is the additional concern that television may be "grinding us down to spiritual dust so fine that a puff of wind scatters it, leaving nothing behind," according to Malcolm Muggeridge.

Very few people take such concerns to heart. Most of

us assume that television is like the weather: We complain about it but don't believe that it can be changed. Some Americans go cold turkey, giving away their television sets, but there is no major movement afoot, even among Christians, to renounce television. We still complain about television, but we have resigned ourselves to television's being an enormous industry over which we have little control.

I must admit that the television industry will not easily be persuaded to change its ways. The American television business is governed largely by ratings and advertising revenues, not by spiritual, artistic, or moral guidelines. "In America, television can make so much money doing its worst, it cannot afford to do its best," said former producer Fred Friendly. Any significant change in television programming in the United States would come about only as a result of a change of heart of the media moguls who run the networks and their parent companies. The Federal Communications Commission, which is supposed to regulate broadcasting in the "public interest, convenience, and necessity," no longer really regulates programming. While cable television offers more channels, it, too, is big business. Cable offers some marvelous cultural programs, exciting sports events, and even many worthwhile Hollywood films, but also provides some of the most morally objectionable and spiritually degrading shows ever shown on television. Cable does not redeem television; it merely gives us more of the very best and very worst programming available, along with heavy doses of the typically ridiculous and mundane.

In my judgment, public broadcasting most deserves the support of Christians who value worthwhile television entertainment and information. Although public television is not produced specifically for the Christian community, neither is it a pulpit for secular humanists to preach their own gospel, as some have claimed. In spite of the clearly secular perspective of programs such as Carl Sagan's "Cosmos," public broadcasting represents a wide variety of political, cultural, and religious perspectives. Moreover, public broadcasters are far more committed than commercial broadcasters to offering interesting, provocative, and engaging programming. They aired worthwhile children's programs when the networks considered it socially responsible to replay endlessly a battery of old cartoons. Public television also kept alive the documentary program and anthology series long after the commercial networks discarded them in favor of evening soap operas and police shows. And cooperation between public broadcasting and foreign producers, especially the BBC and Granada Television, keeps American television from becoming thoroughly ethnocentric. Public television stations are also one of the few broadcast sources of foreign news and drama. We should watch public television just as critically as we do the commercial networks, but as a general rule, public stations offer artistically superior and morally better programming.

A few local churches and national denominations encourage members to boycott sponsors of morally objectionable or blasphemous programs. Donald Wildmon of the Coalition for Better Television supplies hundreds of concerned churches and thousands of individuals with program evaluations and sponsor addresses. His newsletter also reprints transcripts from some of the more offensive programs. The coalition's efforts are a step in the right direction, coalescing support from Christians of many different theological backgrounds. But too often, advertisers and the networks receive only critical letters dealing with sex and violence. If we boycott advertisers or complain to networks, we ought also to encourage them when the programs aired are especially worthwhile. And we ought not to let our criticism focus only on a show's immorality, since such letters frequently only support a network's stereotype of the typical prudish evangelical.

Regardless of the source of our television program— cable, network, public—we still must use television Christianly. The problem is not only what to watch but also when and how much to watch. Even if the quality of television programming were improved, we might still find television negatively affecting our lives. The church, the school, and the family all have responsibilities for helping us to use television Christianly.

During the last fifteen years, terms such as "electronic church" and "electric church" have been used to describe the relationship between television and the church. These expressions do capture some of what happened to Christianity in the United States: A number of well-known and effective evangelists used the airways to establish a new kind of church without walls, personal fellowship, and often accountability. While much could be said about these religious broadcasters, the purpose of this final section is to describe and evaluate the opportunities that the local congregation has to help its members to use television Christianly.

I have discovered in recent years that most Christians genuinely desire to use television in God-glorifying ways, but they sense that the task is too complicated to

undertake alone. More Christian homemakers, for example, are struggling with television as a baby-sitter in
their homes. They are also concerned about television
violence and about their own viewing habits. Lacking
any immediate advice or solutions, however, they continue using television as they have in the past.

The local church is probably the best place for
concerned Christians to begin discussing how to use the
media constructively. I have addressed many Christian
women's groups who have shared with me many of the
practical suggestions offered in these final chapters. I go
to some of these meetings expecting to lecture to the
homemakers and leave with the feeling that I have
learned more from my hosts. Too often we view the
congregation as a group who meets only for Sunday
worship and weekday Bible studies. The church is really
a community of believers who instruct and encourage
one another in the faith, a group of sinful but redeemed
followers of Christ who exercise their gifts for the benefit
of the church and the entire society. We need not only
meet to study the Word but also to discuss how the Word
applies to our lives as well. Sunday school classes, adult
education sessions, youth groups, retreats, household
prayer groups—these are all opportunities to share ideas
about using television Christianly.

If you are unsure about how to organize or lead a local
meeting to discuss television, ask a speaker from the
community to speak to your church group. Perhaps there
is a Christian college in your area; invite one of the
communications faculty to address an adult Sunday
school class or youth group. I don't know of any such
faculty who would refuse such an offer! Most of them
have rather strong views about the media and their

impact on the church, the school, and the family. Choose as a topic for the lecture a common concern among parents in your area, e.g., How to set family viewing standards, or Should Christians subscribe to cable TV? Ask friends in other churches if they know of any Christians who work at a local television station, who might come to your church to discuss the financial and ethical aspects of broadcasting. Although one cannot tell from watching television, there are evangelicals in the media, especially at local stations. Frequently, they share with viewers some of the concerns about television's impact on our nation and culture. Their insights are often helpful, and their anecdotes about the media are usually entertaining.

Pastors have special opportunities for instructing the congregation about television. Television shows—plots, characters, and settings—are valuable examples for illustrating sermon ideas. Among Christians, television stories are probably better known than even Bible stories. Imagine a sermon that contrasts the Godly qualities of Peter or David with the modern-day heroism of Matt Dillon or Rockford! Which people are the real, Christian heroes? Or consider a sermon contrasting biblical love, as represented in God and human acts of self-sacrifice, with media renditions of romantic love. No marriage could survive television's versions of love, where two people are not committed, but infatuated. Similarly compelling might be a sermon or Bible study that looks at both scriptural and televisual notions of justice. What would Madison Avenue say about the Beatitudes? Are the poor and the oppressed really to be blessed? Any sermon about sin could refer to the almost complete absence of any mention of it on the tube, since the notion that man is evil is simply not popular these days. Similarly, there is almost no sense of God or any transcendent being in television shows.

If television really captures some of the most popular myths and heroes of our time, pastors who use the tube for examples are helping to build spiritual discernment in an age that truly requires it.

The church badly needs a prophetic critique of the media. It needs sermons that distinguish between television's presentations of God's grace and its self-serving depictions of mankind's ability to solve its own problems and eradicate evil. Even more than this, the church should encourage its teachers and preachers to reveal television's perspectives on life, for the tube's point of view is also our own culture's point of view. When we watch television, we see something of ourselves hidden behind the glittery celebrities and unrealistic stories. But the reflection is not perfect; it becomes clearer as our contemporary prophets paint its contours with biblical colors.

Finally, the church needs internal television critics, people who write about television for congregations, denominations, and individual Christians. Critics can compare programs and series for us, tell us what new programs are worth watching, and help us determine which shows are worthwhile for young children and teens. They can give pastors and Sunday school instructors suggestions about using television programs for illustrations of human depravity and God's redemption. They can even bring pressure to bear on the networks, stations, and sponsors by encouraging us to write letters about particularly outstanding or especially objectionable shows. We may not always agree with our own

Christian critics, but we need their prophetic voice in our denominational and independent evangelical publications. If your favorite Christian publication does not have a television review column, drop a note to the editor suggesting that one be started. Even a well-written column is bound to be controversial and sometimes a headache for the editor, but it is also likely to be one of the most widely read sections of the publication.

But the church will still not significantly soften the impact of television on its members until it addresses the role of the medium in our lives. Because television viewing is free and effortless, millions of Americans have made it their major leisure activity. They depend upon the tube for nightly entertainment, weekly sports, daily news, and even dinner distraction. For many of us television is a substitute for community, a perverted and unfulfilling activity we do when we should be building *koinonia*. For others of us television is the blessed baby-sitter who never tires and is always available. Regardless of what we watch, we probably watch too much.

The local church, the community of believers that meets in fellowship, must encourage and strengthen the bonds that hold its members together. Surely we share the common bond of Christ, who was sacrificed for us all. Yet we should share our lives as well—our trials and tribulations, our happiness and joy, our musings and dreams. In short, we must do as followers of Christ the very thing that television threatens to monopolize: We must share with each other our stories about life, God's grace, and His marvelous Creation. As we meet in friendship for worship, prayer, and play, our faith becomes one, and we reflect to the world the fruits of the greatest story of all the salvation of God's people. One task of the local congregation, then, is to help believers communicate authentically with each other, not privately with the television set.

In addition, the church ought to provide resources and people to assist members whose lifestyles create an unhealthy dependence on television. Especially needy in today's society are senior citizens and single parents, contemporary versions of what scripture often calls the poor and the widowed. The elderly watch far more television than others in America primarily because they often feel unwanted by family, church, and community. The church should be more creative at using the gifts and talents of its more experienced members, and church programs ought to address their interests and needs. Single parents, on the other hand, are often oppressed by the multiple burdens of parenting, working, and housekeeping. For them television is an easy but often unsatisfactory way of defusing the pressure to attend to the children. Surely the church ought to help by sharing time and love with the children and the parent. We must provide alternatives to television.

If television is "manna from Hollywood," as this book suggests, the church is needed to proclaim the true food that humankind hungers for. The church is not just the professional clergy, but you and I and every believer. We serve spiritual food each time we act in the name of the Lord to release friends and neighbors from the bondage of television.

10

Television and the School

Teachers are especially critical of television. If you have school-age children, talk with your child's teachers about the effects of television. Most teachers will tell you of their own experiences with hyperactive and slow-learning children who watch a lot of television. They see an obvious connection between the educational abilities of children and television viewing. I recently listened to a concerned high-school drawing instructor recall that over the last twenty years, the ability of students to sketch a simple figure has progressively worsened—a problem he attributed to television viewing. A third-grade teacher told me that she knew how violent or visually stimulating a previous night's television programs were by how hyperactive the students were the next morning. Obviously these are anecdotal lessons, not scientific explanations of the effects of television.

Social scientists have not been able to determine the

precise effects of television on children or adults, and my guess is that they never will. Individuals' susceptibility to television varies enormously. For example, even though student surveys show that students who watch five or six hours of television per day generally are poor readers, the scientists cannot conclude that television viewing itself is the cause. Some studies have even concluded that a child's academic abilities are influenced less by how much he watches than by what he watches. There are hundreds of often contradictory studies that often say more about the preoccupations of the researchers than the significance of television. Instead of waiting for sociologists or psychologists to tell the schools what to do about television, we simply have to respond to the medium's apparent influence based on our own experiences.

My concern is that the secondary schools are doing very little to build visual literacy among students. Educators rightly point out that television is primarily the responsibility of the parents, not the schools. But even if the parents grapple seriously with television viewing in the home, there is still much work to be done teaching students how to be as critical of visual tales as they are of written stories. English classes teach reading, writing, and eventually literature but usually pay scant attention to films and television programs. By the end of high school, the typical student may have read and analyzed dozens of novels and short stories but never have critically examined a single film or videotape. Art courses teach some rudimentary understanding of visual aesthetics but typically ignore the major visual medium—television.

Perhaps secondary schools should direct at least a

small part of the curriculum toward the goal of creating visual literacy among students. Frankly, I think the Christian schools are best equipped, since they can address religious issues and themes more openly and directly. Christian young people need not only to understand how television works but also how to evaluate the themes and myths of popular television programming. Even the public schools can address both of these objectives, although there may be considerable resistance from some parents and school administrators about getting too heavily involved in evaluating program content.

A Christian high school I visited boldly introduced a six-week course about the media, particularly film and television. While parents were not fully supportive of the new course at the beginning, they eventually saw its value in helping their families to discuss television programs and popular movies. As the children brought home for discussion various issues and problems related to the media, parents began assessing their own viewing habits.

A number of schools have instituted week- or month-long media-awareness programs, sponsored by parent-teacher associations, during which the families of school children voluntarily refrain from watching television or viewing films. Not surprisingly, it's often the parents who complain most strongly about such programs, since they have to think of other activities for their children. Short-term media courses build family awareness of the growing role of television in American life, but they usually fail to change people's viewing habits and lifestyles. Probably the best approach to media studies in the schools is to integrate principles of visual literacy into a variety of standard subjects, including government, religion, social studies, English, and history. For example, a government course might study some of the advertising techniques used to create candidate images during an election. A religion course could compare biblical heroes, such as David and Peter, with the stereotyped, superhuman heroes of a popular television series. English teachers might show students a public television's adaptation of a great novel after they have read and discussed it. Local television stations usually will supply speakers to schools. Don't settle for someone from the station's public-relations department, however; ask for a station executive or program producer. And don't be afraid to recommend a topic, such as how stations decide which programs to broadcast.

Parents sometimes oppose media studies in schools because they don't think that their children are watching too much television or going to the wrong kinds of films. In reality, parents typically don't know what their children are really watching. A survey of the students at a conservative, Midwest, Christian high school recently determined that the most frequently seen film was "Porky's," a popular teen "sexploitation" movie of the eighties. Many of the students who would not go to movie theaters saw the film at home on their parent's VCR or on cable television.

The new technologies are greatly expanding the opportunity for teens to view adult films and television programs without risking getting caught. A growing fad among teens is the video party, where friends gather in a house where the parents are away to view an R- or X-rated videotape rented from a local shop or copied off of cable.

TELEVISION: MANNA FROM HOLLYWOOD?

Sneaking a peek at an X-rated film on the home television is much like secretly puffing on a cigarette behind the garage; teens today see both as activities they must experience before becoming an adult. Unlike cigarettes, however, television shows and films tell stories about life. Young people watch an awful lot of artistic and moral garbage on television and screen. This garbage has become increasingly important in forming young people's identities. Teens were self-conscious about their clothes and their language long before television came along, but never have teens looked more seriously to the tube for cues on what to wear and what to say. Today a program like "Miami Vice" can set the style for much contemporary fashion. Many teenagers are like transparent seedlings, reflecting in themselves the latest media-generated cultural tastes that nourish their identities for good and bad.

As the popularity of MTV indicates, television is one of the most manipulative of all media. Rock videos and many television shows and commercials encourage viewers to experience the shows, not to think about them. Such visually oriented programs as "Miami Vice" are the worst offenders. Even parents and educators often watch television uncritically in their own homes. If the schools are to have a central role in creating a sensitivity in students about the visually manipulative media, they must provide opportunities for discussing and evaluating specific television dramas and other types of shows. Critical television viewing must be learned, just as young people must learn to read critically.

Unlike many television critics, I don't support the widespread use of television in elementary schools. As I see it, visual literacy is dependent upon students' ability to read and to write. If a child cannot first organize and express his thoughts, if he is unable to develop a thesis logically and carefully, he does not have the necessary skills for critiquing a television program or film. Nor am I convinced that so-called educational television materials are typically very valuable in the elementary classroom, although I have seen some that integrate well with more traditional curricula. Certainly all of the hoopla fifteen years ago about the great, impending benefits of classroom television instruction was misguided optimism. Elementary instruction is still a lot of hard work, requiring much individualized help and attention from teachers. Moreover, successful elementary instruction must emphasize social as well as intellectual development. School activities that encourage television viewing are likely to deter social development even at home; admittedly, this can be a problem in elementary curricula that overemphasize other private activities as well, such as personal computing and even reading.

The schools can also help reverse the growing passivity of children raised in the television age. Television encourages people to be consumers of life, not active and well-informed participants in the world. As one educator said, "Television is an appliance which [can] change children from irresistible forces into immovable objects." In the United States, watching television has become the great metaphor for how the nation tends to approach life. "It's a little weird when you have the whole country watching a couple of people doing what they should be doing themselves," joked one talk-show producer. In this television age we see ourselves largely as spectators of the world around us, and we often fail to lead, to organize, and to shape. God's commandment in Genesis

TELEVISION: MANNA FROM HOLLYWOOD?

1 that we responsibly take dominion over His Creation is one of the clearest and strongest of the Scriptures. We are the Lord's servants, caring for and developing the earth on His behalf. The Creation is meant to be enjoyed, but it is also meant to be cultivated for its riches and preserved for its Creator and future generations. I'm repeatedly amazed by my own former students who, several years after graduation, write to tell me that they are surprised that their efforts actually can make a difference in the world. Apparently, they believe that only fictional heroes can affect change in neighborhoods, states, and nations.

Popular television programming encourages us to become passive audiences awaiting the latest commercial messages and political propaganda. Few programs really foster thoughtful viewing. During a presidential election year, I sometimes ask my students to write down everything they know for fact about the candidate they support. Rarely do I get more than several short paragraphs, much of which is nonfactual. In modern society, it is so easy for all of us to base our prejudices and stereotypes on the messages whipped together by the tube.

School curricula that engage the student in what is going on outside of the classroom have the best chance of breaking the passivity of children in our television society. Field trips and extracurricular activities, such as sports and music, are extremely important in building students' self-esteem. Children who watch a lot of television are far less likely to be involved in church and civic projects. As adults they might be less inclined to serve on school boards, civic organizations, or church committees. Without the help of a school system that teaches them to be active and responsible citizens, students will contentedly sit in the ever-present glow of the television set.

Until recently, most parents and pastors have discouraged college students from pursuing careers in the media. They wisely feared that media-related work might create a worldly attitude among their young people, who could get caught up in the glamour and carnality of the personality-oriented business. Certainly more than one well-intentioned young adult has wandered away from the church and the faith by entering the visually seductive world of television. But over the years broadcasting has changed considerably, and at the same time the world itself has become more like television. Just as there are many different law firms espousing alternative practices and ethics, so, too, is there a wider choice of media-related occupations and careers. Cable television and satellites have increased the number of television channels. Now there are nearly a dozen religious channels available nationally. Special channels exist for sports, news, films, health information, various ethnic groups, weather reports, and even financial data. While the major commercial networks—ABC, NBC, and CBS—still dominate television in the United States, their power is slowly being eroded by the growing number of cable competitors, low-power community television stations, various other pay-television operations, and especially the VCR. Christians involved in these new media have the chance to influence their development, and the high schools ought to encourage talented students to pursue media careers cautiously, but committedly.

Let's encourage our colleges to offer courses dealing with the artistic, spiritual, and ethical aspects of television. The media are the Lord's, and students with the appropriate gifts and abilities ought to be assured by teachers, counselors, and parents that television or any other medium is not inherently worldly and evil. Ironically, during the formative years of American television, when many of the shows were far less morally objectionable and more carefully crafted than they are today, Christian young people feared to go into media careers. Now that the evil and corrupt aspects of broadcasting have taken root, a growing number of parents and their children are seriously considering entering media professions. Our young people can have a major impact on the developing media if they are not discouraged as they were in the fifties and sixties. If they are to access and reform the media, however, they need a liberal-arts education, not narrowly technical degrees offered by many colleges and universities.

The schools have an important role to play in helping students and society to use television appropriately and effectively. They can help cultivate critical viewing and, in the Christian colleges and universities, explore ways of redeeming the medium for Christ.

11

Television and the Home

Television was invited into the American home in the late forties, and it has never left. Uncle Charlie comes and goes with the various holidays, birthdays, and reunions, but the television sits in the family room undisturbed, except for the occasional trips to the repairman. Toddlers eventually become five-year-olds, who go off to kindergarten; the television set greets them every day after school. Maturing young people frequently leave home for college but return during vacations to catch up on their favorite shows as well as to visit with kinfolk and peers. Television is a strange source of stability for our families. The shows change, but the bluish glow of the television remains in the contemporary family.

An American household has the set on an average of about seven hours daily. Adults watch television for two or three of those hours, and children sit in front of the set for about four hours each day. While some parents say that television actually keeps the family together, the evidence suggests the contrary: Parents spend about a half-hour per day viewing television programs with their children. To make matters worse, parents generally spend very little time in non-television viewing activities with their children. Mothers who work outside of the home spend only about eleven minutes each weekday, and homemakers only about a half-hour each day, in child-related activities. Fathers spend eight minutes on weekdays and fourteen minutes a day on weekends doing things with their children.

An informal survey of young boys conducted a few years ago came to some startling conclusions about television viewing. Ninety percent of the boys said that they would rather watch their favorite show than spend the time playing with their fathers. Perhaps fathers are somewhat to blame for their sons' preference; most fathers would agree that they should give more attention to their children. But the lure of the television is strong for young boys, who especially like the aggressive characters and automobile violence of the action shows.

Television programming is not created with the intention of encouraging families to watch. The networks broadcast shows to maximize the total number of sets tuned in, not the number of families viewing. In fact, the program rating system is based on the concept of "household" viewing, which means the number of houses with a set on, not the number of families watching those sets. Program writers rarely consider whether a program will be enjoyed by a family or whether it is even appropriate for a family. Instead they think narrowly of the ratings that a show might achieve. One adult and one family are the same in the ratings.

Since it is easier to attract individual viewers than to produce shows that will attract entire families, very few family oriented programs are ever produced.

Families who do watch television together generally do not communicate while viewing. Television probably interrupts opportunities for genuine family discussion more than it fosters them. It tends to make our thoughts and feelings for each other even more private. We sit together in the same room, but we focus our attention on television, not on each other. A television is a great source of local news and information in the kitchen when dinner is being prepared, but the same set disrupts mealtime discussion if it's not turned off. Even our furniture is arranged for comfortable viewing rather than for fellowship and conversation. The idea that a family viewing time is necessarily good for a family is one of the great misunderstandings of the nature of the television medium. Instead of communicating with each other, most families who view the tube together actually grow increasingly distant from one another. They learn about television, not about themselves and their kin. Personal needs and concerns go overlooked as the family focuses its attention on the characters on the tube. Family members cannot serve one another unless they know one another well, and television viewing usually is not used to build such close relationships.

The older and newer media technologies tend to break apart the family, sending each child and parent off to their own set. Television thrives on families who rarely spend time together playing games, vacationing, participating in local sports, and simply talking. Oddly enough, Sundays are the prime rating days on commercial networks. This day in our society, because of religious tradition, has provided the most leisure time and has made the "Ed Sullivan Show" and "60 Minutes" two of the most successful programs ever broadcast. Now Sunday afternoons bring us highly profitable sports events, especially football. Many wives are discouraged by their husbands' excessive viewing of professional football on the Lord's Day—the one day when many husbands are home. Wives rightly complain when their husbands spend little time talking with their spouses and four hours glaring at the television on Sunday afternoons. Even the family dinner, once a time for family discussion, is now sometimes interrupted by television game shows, news, and sports.

Television is at least partly responsible for the generation gap. Families who do not spend adequate time together building warm and loving relationships are likely to drift off into selfish ways of life. MTV beckons the teen viewer; Sunday football lures the sports-fan father; soaps attract the homemaker. Television offers a little something for everyone, but little for the family. Anthropologist Margaret Mead believes that in American society young people today learn far more from their peers than they do from their own parents and extended families. She argues that this major transformation of society makes it extremely difficult for parents and grandparents to pass on their values and beliefs to the youth. Teens, for example, spend more time listening to other teens and watching their favorite teen idols on television than they do discussing life with their own parents. As a result, teens feel like they live in a different world than the one of their parents; parents appear old-fashioned and ignorant about the ways of the world. Teens slowly break off communication with parents and even younger brothers and sisters, while diving deeper into the media world of radio, television, and film.

The spread of cable and the domestic use of video-cassette recorders (VCRs) have created new ways of using television that further interfere with family communication. Cable provides programming for specific audiences—hourly news and weather, "religious" broadcasts, business reports, specialized sports reporting, adult oriented drama, nonstop children's programming, round-the-clock country music, and rock videos on MTV and its competitors. Each of these types of programming is designed to attract only a particular segment of the American viewing public. They are generally far less family oriented than even traditional network broadcasting. And videocassette recorders, for all of their advantages, have created a new breed of television addict—the person who can't stand to miss a television program or a Hollywood film that was originally presented at a time when he was busy. While VCRs potentially enable us to use our leisure time more efficiently, they actually encourage many people to fill up their leisure time with visual entertainment. Many worthwhile children's programs and family-oriented films are available on video-tape, but few parents use the technology carefully to build family life. Too often we subscribe to cable or purchase a VCR without any clear idea about how we will use them. As a result, we end up letting the new technologies rearrange our own priorities.

Admittedly, television is not the only problem. Any activities that involve only individual family members potentially divide the family unit. One congregation to which my family belonged hoped to build family life by establishing Wednesday evenings at church as "family night." Every week most of the families rushed through dinner, jumped in their cars and rushed over to church, only to be split into different groups by age and interest! As I told the pastor, this was not a family night, but another evening where the parents and children went in separate directions.

Families that replace some of their television viewing with more rewarding and creative forms of play are more likely to love and serve one another. Even such simple activities as walks and picnics are wonderful vehicles for building family life. Parents usually realize when they have to get away from the kids for an evening to chat over dinner or during a walk; less obvious is the need for a family to gather together. Some families go camping together—without the television. Others have a family time every evening after dinner, playing games that all ages enjoy. I usually take my seven-year-old son along on Saturday trips to the hardware store, even though the errands often take twice as long. Hardware stores bring out the curiosity in even the most reserved children. Parents of teens find it helpful to take turns washing the dishes with individual children after dinner; the rest of the family scatters, but personal discussion between the parent and child is encouraged. Could it be that as we are becoming increasingly professional television viewers, we are turning into amateur parents and children? If so, it could be partly because of television's role as a baby-sitter in the home. Parents wrongly assume that television is worthwhile solely because it baby-sits children and keeps teens off the street. We ought instead to consider whether our use of television really helps create a meaningful family life in our homes.

In a growing number of homes, parents and children

set a specific limit on the amount of television that may be watched by family members each day. Sometimes parents limit their children's television viewing based on school grades; for example, as grades improve, the child may view more television programs per day or week. One or two hours of viewing won't initially elicit cheers from the children, especially if they are used to watching three or four hours daily. In the long run, however, children whose viewing time is curtailed will happily take up new hobbies and interests. Many studies reveal that parents, not children, have the most difficult time adjusting to life without unlimited television viewing. Parents who often see television as the only source of relaxation after a hectic day must relearn the basic skills of conversation, play, and relaxation. In our home the television is normally on no longer than one hour daily. Exceptions are when videocassettes are rented for the family, major sports events, and special network programs such as documentaries and non-series drama.

Perhaps television's most unapparent influence is the medium's impact on our spiritual lives. Personal prayer, meditation, and reflection are difficult for all of us in the television age. We're losing grasp of the importance of silence and solitude in our relationships with God and each other. The sights and sounds of the time are constantly distracting our minds and hearts from spiritual matters. If for no other reason, we ought to limit our television viewing to spend time praying and studying God's Word. When we are at peace with God, we will more likely be living in harmony with those around us, including our families. My wife and I decided to cultivate our five-year-old son's spiritual life partly by establishing his own daily quiet time, during which he cannot play with friends or watch television. He enjoys the hour in his room, working alone on crafts or simply resting. Although some of his quiet time projects involve Christian themes, we don't require that he spend the entire hour or so on spiritual matters. The idea is simply to encourage him to develop and appreciate a quiet time, which the Spirit may use in the years ahead to build him into a prayerful and meditative servant of God.

Once the amount of television watched in our homes is under control and we have replaced some of our viewing with other family activities, it's time to consider how to determine which programs are worth watching. By openly discussing standards for selecting shows, parents can help build spiritual discernment among their children. If parents dogmatically refuse to allow their kids to watch various programs, the gap between the lifestyles and values of parents and children is likely to grow. But if parents and children together discuss why particular shows are unacceptable or worthwhile, both can improve their spiritual discernment and deepen their personal relationships. At first there is likely to be a struggle; especially teens will feel that the discussions are meant to lecture them on the evils of television. But these perceptions can be overcome if parents are truly open to the ideas and experiences of their children. In short, such discussion of television must be handled with a spirit of love and acceptance.

Families that limit television viewing must make choices: Which show shall we watch? Which is the best show? Which programs are we willing to sacrifice? Why? Which shows are most appropriate for the family? Too many families never address these choices, instead opting to purchase enough television sets to satisfy everyone in the house. Families that view television together must learn to negotiate and compromise, since only one program can be watched at a time. In multiple-child families, the problem of which child's favorite show to watch can actually be turned into a lesson of self-sacrifice. Probably the best time to begin such discussions is just before the beginning of a fall television season. Several evenings can be set aside for the family to review newspaper descriptions of the new programs, and a schedule of family viewing can be established. Without such discussions the normal tendency in families is to argue while a program is being watched. Tempers flare and regrettable words are exchanged by both parents and children.

I recall a middle-aged father who once complained to me in an adult church class about his teenage daughter who insistently asked that she be allowed to watch a daytime soap opera. He wanted to know how he could convince her not to watch the show. "Why does she want to watch a soap opera?" I asked him in front of the group. "Beats me," he replied. "Have you ever discussed sex with her?" I further asked. He turned red but didn't answer. At that point it was clear to everyone in the room where I was going with the question: Young people frequently watch soaps and go to teen oriented films to learn about sex and adulthood. Puberty is a time of great personal insecurity when young people are grappling with what it means to be an adult. This teenage girl probably wanted to watch soaps because they were one way for her to find out about the adult world—at least to find out about how television depicts adults sexually. I suggested to the frustrated father that perhaps he ought to watch and discuss the soap opera with his daughter.

They could consider how soaps depict sexuality and how such depictions differ from a Christian perspective. The group snickered at the thought of a middle-aged father watching soaps with his young daughter, but as our discussion continued, everyone seemed to agree that this father's problem was not simply how to control the television set but how to create the kind of relationship with his daughter that would lead to an open and loving discussion of sex and marriage.

One evening after leading a discussion about MTV with Christian teenagers, I was approached by a quiet girl who was obviously upset. She explained that her parents refused to let her watch MTV, so she would go to a friend's house to "study" in the evening. The two of them watched their favorite rock videos in the privacy of her friend's bedroom. Her guilt about lying to her parents was a heavy burden on her soul, and she had come to me for advice. She felt trapped because her parents refused to discuss their MTV ban with her. Not surprisingly, her parents had never watched MTV, even though they subscribed to cable. The parents' uninformed and dogmatic attitude toward MTV was slowly destroying their relationship with the guilt-ridden daughter. At stake in the battle over television viewing was nearly all communication between the girl and her parents.

Discussing television programs as a family can lead to deeper conversations about how to live the Christian life. As the earlier chapters have shown, television programs are far more than simple-minded entertainment. They say something about America, about our heroes, and about the nature of good and evil. Like all plays and novels, television programs are stories that reflect something of the people who create them as well as say something about the people who enjoy them. Some situation comedies are excellent stories for talking as a family about things that make us laugh. Detective shows are sometimes worth discussing from the perspective of Christian justice and mercy. Even children's television, such as "Mister Rogers' Neighborhood," deals with issues of great importance to our youngsters. Fred Rogers' shows are excellent opportunities for parents and children to discuss such common feelings as anger, self-esteem, friendships, love. When we look at all television merely as idle entertainment, we lose the opportunity to use it for instruction and spiritual development. In my home the television set is in a corner of the family room, where it can be seen by everyone working in the kitchen. While preparing dinner or enjoying a cup of tea in the eating area, my wife and I are always able to see what's on television and when appropriate, to discuss it with the children afterward.

Parents set an example for the family by their own viewing habits and program preferences. Young children generally want to be like their parents and will imitate the parents' actions. Teens, on the other hand, see immediately any hypocrisy in the difference between what parents say about television and what they actually do with the television. Parents who complain about television sex and violence or who criticize their children for watching mindless programs must be prepared to adjust their own viewing habits accordingly. No father who watches only action shows, such as "Dukes" and "A-Team," can easily convince a teenage son that there are better programs on television.

Regardless of the quality of programming, we should never let viewing television become a substitute for reading in the home. Children of all ages benefit from a parent's voice sparking their imagination through verse, rhyme, and story. And literate children can take their turns reading to the rest of the family. Much Christian writing is admittedly unimaginative and lifeless, but there is a worthwhile body of fantasy literature to keep any Christian family joyfully entertained on cold winter evenings and lazy summer afternoons. Try reading aloud the fantasy books of C. S. Lewis and J. R. R. Tolkien.

The thoughtless and indiscriminate use of television in the home is a problem in America, but it is also an opportunity for each family to examine itself and to establish new priorities. In the Bible the family is more than a collection of individuals carrying out their specialized tasks in the home. God uses the family to stabilize and order society and, more than that, to carry out his redemptive plan. We are not just to raise children, but to raise them in the Lord. Church and family together raise up each new generation of witnesses for Christ and workers in His kingdom. If television stands in the way of these tasks, then we ought to look at how the trend might be reversed. By replacing some of our viewing with more socially and spiritually rewarding activities, and by openly establishing family viewing criteria, we are well on the way to redeeming our use of the great storyteller of our time.